1848 in France

DOCUMENTS OF REVOLUTION
General Editor: Heinz Lubasz

1848 in France

EDITED BY ROGER PRICE

Cornell Paperbacks
CORNELL UNIVERSITY PRESS
Ithaca, New York

FRONTISPIECE: *'Defenders of the
Barricade'. The victors of February,
National Guard, bourgeois and worker,
portrayed by Gavarni.*

*Documents translated by C. N. Smith
Picture research by Alla Weaver*

First published 1975

*International Standard Book Number 0-8014-9149-5
Library of Congress Catalog Card Number 74-11607*

Printed in Great Britain

Contents

ITRODUCTION   11

ART ONE: FEBRUARY–JUNE 1848

The Development of a Revolutionary Situation   52
The Revolution Successful   62
Measures of the Provisional Government   68
The Promise of a New Era for the Workers   72
The Conservative Conception of the Republic   73
The Call for Continuous Public Action   73
Radical Republican Proposals for Action   74
Workers' Demands   75
Revolutionary Republicanism   76
Petition for the Postponement of the Election of a Constituent
Assembly   77
Conservative Fears   77
The Creation of a Conservative Alliance   79
The Moderate Republican Desire for Order   80
The Provisional Government Frightens Conservatives   80
The Forty-Five-Centime Tax   80
Popular Disorder in the Provinces   81
Popular Demonstrations in Paris: 17 March 1848   84
The Election Campaign   85
The Clergy and the Elections   92
Popular Indifference   93
Weakness of the Republican Electoral Campaign   93
The Election   94
Election Results   95
Election Results and Reactions to Them   96
Paris at the End of April 1848   96
The Left Organizes   97
Republicans and the Constituent Assembly   97
Government Preparations to Suppress Disorder   98
The Demonstration of 15 May 1848   98

30 Demands for a Showdown 100
31 Agitation and Organization in Paris 100
32 Strikers in Paris 100
33 National Workshops 101
34 A Symptom of Discontent: Bonapartism 105
35 Murmurs of Insurrection 105

PART TWO: THE JUNE INSURRECTION

1 The Beginnings of Insurrection 107
2 Military Tactics 109
3 Barricades in Paris 109
4 The Course of Insurrection 110
5 Reasons for Insurrection 110
6 Sympathetic Response in the Provinces 112
7 Fear in the Provinces 112
8 In Defence of Society 113
9 The Brutality of Repression 114
10 Marseilles: Demonstration of 22 June 114
11 Conservative Explanation of the June Insurrection 115
12 Radical Republicans: Legalism and Realism 116
13 Disillusioned Republicans 116
14 In Defence of Civilization 117

PART THREE: JUNE 1848 – MAY 1849

1 Political Alignments and Re-alignments 118
2 Political Polarization 118
3 Political Repression 119
4 Political Isolation of the Constituent Assembly 120
5 The Need for Moral Order 120
6 The God of Property 121
7 Conservative Fears Unallayed 121
8 Rumour or Reality? 121
9 The Threat Remains 122
10 Need for Strong Government 122
11 Official Recognition of the Danger 122
12 The Socialists Reorganize 123
13 Continuing Social Unrest 124
14 Radical Republicanism Moves Leftward 126
15 The Conservative Republic 127
16 Debate on the Constitution: Powers of the President of the Republic 127

7 Conservative Contempt for Parliamentarians   127
8 The Presidential Elections   128
9 The Appeal of the Conservative Bonaparte   131
0 General Cavaignac's Candidature   131
1 Anti-Bonapartist Propaganda   131
2 The People go to the Polls   132
3 Louis-Napoléon Bonaparte: Prince President of the Republic 133
4 Conservative Unity in Defence of their Republic   133
5 The Old Parties Survive   134
6 Elections to the Legislative Assembly   134
7 Growing Appeal of a Bonapartist Solution   136
8 Conservatives Move Right   136

PART FOUR: MAY 1849 – DECEMBER 1851

1 Further Political Polarization: Moderate Republicans Move
   Leftward   137
2 Radical Republican Demonstration: 13 June 1849   138
3 Disorder in Lyon: Government Response   139
4 Atmosphere of Unrest   140
5 Radical Demonstration of Strength   140
6 Accident or Social Protest?   140
7 Cholera Epidemic Accentuates the Social Bitterness   140
8 A Radical Republican Celebration   141
9 Preparing for Revolt, or a Means of Avoiding Taxes?   141
0 Conservative Unity and Moral Re-education for the Masses 141
1 Education Law (Loi Falloux) of 1849: Radical Republican Reaction 142
2 Louis-Napoléon the Nation's Hope, Above All Parties   142
3 Dismissal of the Barrot Ministry: Its Significance   143
4 The Weakness of Conservative Resistance to Louis-Napoléon's
   Ambitions   143
5 Early 1850: Conservative View of the Political Situation 143
6 Paris, March 1850: By-election Results   144
7 Growing Anti-parliamentary Feeling   144
8 Republicans in Defence of Universal Suffrage . . .   145
9 . . . Or Not?   145
0 Radical Republican Appeal to the Army   145
1 Order Depends on the Army   146
2 Youthful High Spirits, or Political Threat?   147
3 Radical Organizations Consolidate   147
4 Problems of Repression   148
5 Economic Life: A Crisis of Confidence   149
6 Radical Republican Appeal to Small Property Owners and Workers 149

27 Talk of Revolution 150
28 Official Credence of the Threat of Revolution 151
29 Republicans: Excuses for Inaction and Promise of Action 151
30 The Imperial Pretender 152
31 The Red Spectre 152
32 Call for a Preventive *Coup d'Etat* 153
33 Conservatives Await the *Coup d'Etat* 153

PART FIVE: COUP D'ETAT

1 Early Justifications 154
2 Measures of Repression 155
3 Reactions to the *Coup* 155
4 Resistance in Paris 156
5 Success of the *Coup* in Paris 157
6 Preventive Measures 158
7 The *Coup* at Lyon 158
8 Resistance to the *Coup* 159
9 Waiting on Paris 160
10 Insurrection and Revolt 160
11 Insurgents 169
12 Sung Defiance 170
13 Leaders of Insurrection 170
14 Agitators 171
15 Resistance to the *Coup d'Etat* Became its Justification 174
16 Widespread Indifference 176
17 Demand for MORAL ORDER 177
18 Plebiscite 178
19 *Deo Gratias* 179
20 The Future? 179
21 Revolution and Reaction 180

BIOGRAPHICAL SKETCHES 182

SOURCES OF THE DOCUMENTS 185

SUGGESTED FURTHER READING 187

INDEX 189

SOURCES OF THE ILLUSTRATIONS 192

Acknowledgments

I would like to express my gratitude to the archivists and librarians of the institutions on whose collections of documentary material I drew, and to those of the University College of Wales, Swansea, and the University of East Anglia (whose librarian, Wilhelm Guttsman, and a member of his staff, Barry Taylor, were especially helpful in acquiring material on 1848 in France for the library collection).

Heinz Lubasz not only suggested this book to me but also helped make it a better one than otherwise it might have been. I am grateful to Dr C. N. Smith of the University of East Anglia, who translated the documents, for an easy collaboration; to Stephen Wilson of the same university and to Christopher Johnson of Wayne State University, Detroit, for talking to me about history; to Lynn Lees and Charles Tilly for allowing me to read before its publication their article 'The People of June, 1848'; and to Carol Denmark and Monika Hammond for typing the manuscript undaunted by my horrible handwriting.

Macdonald & Co. kindly allowed me to reproduce passages from the Mayer and Kerr edition of Alexis de Tocqueville's *Recollections*; Editions Gallimard, from J. P. Mayer's edition of the same writer's correspondence; Libraire Plon, from C.-H. Pouthas's edition of Rémusat's memoirs; MM. Pierre Guiral, Raoul Brunon, and the Comité des travaux historiques et scientifiques, of the French Ministère de l'éducation nationale, from the correspondence received by Marshal Pélissier.

My good friends Robert and Jane Frugère helped me in all sorts of ways, and I can never thank them enough. Above all, Heather, Richard and Siân Price made this book possible.

Above, *the departure of a coach, still in 1848 the most rapid form of transport in much of France.*

Left, *'Bringing home the new-born calf' by Millet: the prized possession of a poor family*

Introduction

I

The political events of 1848 in France can be understood only as they occurred within a particular social context. The first part of this introductory essay is therefore given over to a description of French society in 1848. Against that background, the second part analyses political events from the Revolution of February 1848 to the ending of the Republic in December 1852, when Napoleon III was proclaimed Emperor of the French. The course from Revolution to Imperial restoration is charted in relation to the activities of politicians and political groups, and also, more broadly, in terms of the changing balance of power among social groups, examining the degree to which politicians were able to arouse widespread interest in and support for their respective initiatives, and the extent to which the population maintained its traditional apathy, resignation and deference.

The first fact to be aware of is that France was at this time essentially an agricultural country. Because of the physical difficulty of communication between the various geographical regions her economy was under-developed by comparison, for example, with contemporary Britain's. The market for goods of all sorts was limited, a result of the costliness and slowness of transportation, and so there was little call to increase production through technical innovation. In their relative isolation, archaic industries and inefficient agriculture produced mainly for a local market, the chief concern being to ensure local food supplies. Only near large urban areas, and in regions well placed for river or coastal traffic, was there much incentive to meet the demands of a larger market. In fact it would be no exaggeration to describe the France of the 1840s as being based on an economy more usually identified with that under the Ancien Régime: it was still dominated by the agricultural sector and subject to fluctuations according to the size of the harvest, which effectively determined the purchasing power of the population at large and hence affected the demand for industrial products. In this way the harvest influenced urban economies and controlled the level of unemployment, so that town and country alike were dependent on it not only for adequate sustenance but for social peace.

This aspect of the period of Revolution has too often been neglected, but its importance must be appreciated before we can understand French society as it really was in 1848 or comprehend its political behaviour.

Such progress as there was in agricultural techniques before the mid-nineteenth century was essentially limited to clearance and drainage and to the introduction of fodder crops to replace the bare fallow period within the rotation system. Agriculture had become more intensive, but yields remained strikingly low. Even taking into account regional disparities – especially the more rapid rate of advance evident in northern France and in the Paris region – it seems safe to accept the opinion that French agriculture in 1840 was on the whole stagnant, retarded, even primitive. A substantial change in its character took place only after the 1840s, and until then any advance was normally dictated by necessity rather than by agronomists – by demographic pressure imposing a more intensive culture, though with low capital input, as part of the struggle against hunger. Agricultural techniques presupposed an abundance of labour: the inquiry of 1848 revealed that the principal harvesting tool throughout France was still the low-productivity sickle.

It is not always helpful to generalize about crop patterns, but one evident factor was the desire to be self-subsistent. In the resulting polyculture, the kinds of crops varied, but basic foodstuffs, mainly cereals, were always predominant. Some areas, chiefly those with superior communications, were exceptional: the Loire valley, for instance, was able to specialize in a cash crop because the product – wine – could be marketed by river, even though the region's climate and relief were not especially favourable to viticulture. The concentration on cereals resulted in a disequilibrium at the expense of pasture. As a result, the relatively few animals were poor in quality, and the supply of manure was insufficient to permit peasants finally to break away from the old system of crop rotation in which land lay fallow (whether in three-year cycles, as generally in the north, or two-year cycles, as in the south) except in those areas with naturally rich soils, such as Flanders, the Beauce, Alsace and the Limagne. Even in 1840 27 per cent of the cultivable area was in fallow, compared with only 6 per cent in cultivated fodder. The waste of land that this involved, plus the inescapable fact that in some areas as much as a quarter of each crop had to be retained for seeding, imposed severe restrictions on food supply.

The great weakness of the system, however, lay in its transport infrastructure. Communications by water and, particularly, road were slow and costly. Only the first unconnected lines of the future railway network had been constructed before the 1850s. Agricultural prosperity consequently depended on regional market conditions.

Most areas were without the stimulus afforded by a nearby large urban market. Planned division of labour was only possible over very short distances; and substantial price fluctuations were unavoidable in markets, limited in size, when crops varied markedly from year to year according to climatic conditions.

Given this enforced dependence on local supply, grains were grown everywhere. The plains of Languedoc, subsequently given over to vines, were at this time mainly covered with cereals, the vine being largely restricted to hillsides fit for nothing else. An even more graphic representation of the situation could be seen in the terraces, laboriously constructed on hillsides in the Alps and Pyrenees, which were never sufficient to prevent the rain washing away the thin soils so that each year the peasant carried soil back up the hill in panniers strapped to his back.

Peasants were not so much preoccupied with labour productivity as with maximizing the production of food. Given the low yields, there existed at the best of times a frail equilibrium between need and a fluctuating, uncertain level of production. The attitude to agricultural innovation of most of those who farmed the land – and the vast majority were smallholders or tenant-farmers, since relatively few large landowners farmed their land themselves – should be easy to understand. If, with the human geographer Daniel Faucher, we conceive of an agricultural system as an organic whole, as a group of interdependent cultures constituting an equilibrium, then the introduction of new cultures is possible only if substitution of one crop for another does not upset this equilibrium and threaten food supplies. The peasant would require practical proof of this, and it could be provided only by those intellectually and materially able to accept the risk.

The economic historian, Michel Augé-Laribe, has claimed that, in the 'agricultural revolution', the construction of railways was perhaps of even more importance than the introduction of fodder crops. It might not be unfair to say that fear of local shortage, high prices and dearth, and the consequent reluctance to innovate, and to specialize, could only be overcome with the new market structure that came with the creation of a railway network.

But by 1848 such a railway network had made little progress in France: the peasant had not yet been liberated from the constraints of subsistence farming, and population pressure on the land was everywhere increasing.

The signs of relative overpopulation were numerous. They can be detected in the largeness of the area given over to the cultivation of foodstuffs and especially of cereals – an area that drew in more and more marginal land; in the mounting subdivision of the land into ever smaller plots; in increasing indebtedness; in low wages; in low labour productivity; in the great disparity of incomes between social groups; in the low living standards of the mass of people; in the consequences of underemployment and inadequate income – begging and various other ways of supplementing inadequate resources from the land. To pay their taxes, to buy the food they could not grow, to acquire necessities like iron and salt which they could not themselves produce, many of the rural population were forced to seek employment in the industries, particularly textiles, that had been attracted to the countryside by the promise of low labour costs. Others were forced into temporary or seasonal migration.

Adolphe Blanqui, economist brother of the famous revolutionary, concluded from his social inquiries of 1850–51 that 'whatever diversity exists in the soil occupied by these populations, in their habits, in their attitudes, the dominant fact characteristic of their situation is their distress . . . the general inability to satisfy the primary necessities of life'. Consequent upon the demographic and agricultural conditions of the epoch was undernourishment and physical debility – and the low labour productivity resulting from this. Everywhere, ignorance and inadequate water supplies helped breed conditions in which hygiene was lacking and disease flourished.

Social relationships, as well as other elements, in this situation, were both cause and effect within an organic structure. They were fundamentally related to the type of agriculture, dominated by the psychological effects of its inadequacies and by the gross inequalities that resulted from the stuctures of land ownership and use.

Large estates were especially concentrated in the north-west in Normandy, Picardy, the Ile de France and the Loire region, in the valley of the Saône and in the Nivernais, in the south in Languedoc and the Garonne Basin. There were relatively few in the east, in Brittany, the Massif Central; in the Pyrenees and in the Alps. Large estates tended to be found on the plains and

The family of the landowner visits its tenants. Paternalism and submissiveness were vital features of rural life.

Interior of a peasant home in the Landes.

in the valleys where soils were best, rather than in hilly areas where soils were thin and where, because so much manual work was necessary, labour costs were high. The earliest reasonably accurate statistics on land use, from the census reports of 1862 and 1882, indicate that most large proprietors would rather rent their land than directly exploit it, that there were almost two million independent proprietors, almost one and a half million others who either rented or sharecropped land, three million farm servants or day labourers, and one million small property-owners who had of necessity also to work as labourers.

There were perhaps two basic types of society in France before 1848: a democratic type characterized by an equalization of conditions, where most of the land was owned by peasants, and an aristocratic type where various kinds of property and exploitation created a social hierarchy: at its summit was the large landowner, below him the farmer (whether proprietor or tenant) who employed labourers, then the farmer solely dependent on the labour of his family, and finally the labourer (who might often also own a small plot of land). Within a given community the fundamental division was perhaps between those who worked with their hands and those who did not, the former separated by this and by their entire life-style from the mass of the population, as members of the rural bourgeoisie.

These characterizations are obviously of basic types and, of course, variation was infinite between, at the one extreme, the democratic society of the Alps and, at the other, the polarized society of large landowners and farmers and labourers typical of departments like the Seine-et-Oise or Seine-et-Marne.

For most peasants life involved constant insecurity from the threat, or (more accurately) fear, of starvation. This, together with the overpopulation that partly caused it and the geographic isolation in which most of the population lived, helped maintain social relationships based on resignation and deference. These factors and the existence of widespread illiteracy and linguistic particularism ensured that most peasants were unable to imagine any country but their own, and had no standards by which to judge and criticize it. Moreover, they depended on the wealthier members of the community for work and charity. The agricultural system and the societies built on it were in many ways conditioned by the plentiful supply of cheap labour. Often proprietors, aristocrats especially, adopted a genuinely paternalistic attitude toward these populations, reflecting a particular moral conception of social relationships. This was noticeably true in areas like Languedoc and Provence, and above all in the Massif Central and the west, where because of the dispersed character of habitat the population depended on château and church for social cohesion. Although literacy was increasing, those who still enjoyed a monopoly of the kind of education that fitted people to serve as intermediaries between the local society and the outside world – especially the world of officialdom – enjoyed considerable prestige.

If most of the population remained poor, prudent and not openly expressive of their discontent, this did not necessarily mean that they loved the landowners, priests, lawyers and merchants who exploited them. They were well aware of such exploitation, and the elementary antagonism that exists between rich and poor had always been evident. It was always crisis, especially the fear of famine, that recurrently intensified these conflicts. For those who produced a surplus, and sold cereals on the market, a major source of profit was speculation on price movements. These were not only cyclical, but also seasonal, with prices reaching an annual peak in May–mid-August (the end of July in the Midi), the period immediately before harvest. In times of anticipated shortage, merchants and peasants were brought into intense conflict. The various social groups interpreted an economic crisis in different ways, depending on a pre-existing social psychology. The reality of matters was less important that the image men had of it. Evident in particular was a popular misunderstanding of the economic causes of crisis. The tendency was to personalize explanation, to blame speculators cornering supplies, and, in a situation of food shortage to see the increasing long-distance transport of foodstuffs as the proof of this.

In a population living for the most part at subsistence level, any fluctuations in harvests and increases in food prices caused severe hardship. The extent of this varied by region. It was greatest in areas mostly dependent on a single crop. Cereal prices fluctuated least in the Mediterranean area, where imports by sea could be arranged. They were greater in the south-west than in the south-east, and even more evident in the west. All these regions, however, to a greater or lesser extent were areas of polyculture. The centre, east and north were more densely populated, and more dependent on cereals.

Such factors helped determine the character of social relationships. In any particular situation at any specific time, a complex of variables would elicit certain responses. Generalization about cause and effect must be made with caution, and this outline of basic social structures is intended to be no more than suggestive of the whole picture.

Before, and even after the Revolution of 1848, the masses played only a subordinate role in politics. Paternalistic relationships were far more common than oppositions based on class, but in the shaping of politics the exaggerated fears of those who possessed property would play a fundamental part. These fears would to a large extent be created by unrest due to crisis in agriculture. Even the majority of peasants would respond as property owners. Property brought a certain economic security and social prestige. Most men aspired to own it, and their socio-political behaviour, where it was not in support of their demands for 'just' prices, would tend to be in defence of their property against whatever threatened it, whether this was the self-aggrandizing rich man, the tax collector, or the supposed practitioner of communism.

That our present concern with rural society is not exaggerated can be seen from an examination of urban France. In the mid-nineteenth century most urban Frenchmen lived in small market centres that retained close links with the surrounding countryside. The lack of easy and rapid transport meant that each region was cut into small units, each unit having a small town that assumed particular functions as an administrative, marketing and manufacturing centre. The extent to which towns could grow was limited by the range of their activities, and also by the problems of provisioning them – both functions of transport. It could be argued that much of the popular unrest in Paris and Lyon stemmed from the fact that they had outstripped the development of their provisioning facilities and were thus particularly susceptible to price fluctuations.

In this economy, essentially characterized by the high cost of transport and the large proportion of the popular income to be spent on bread, variations in the price of cereals dominated the entire economic cycle. With an increase in food prices, the mass of the population was proportionately less able to purchase industrial goods, resulting in industrial crisis and high unemployment at a time when food prices were rising. The incredible hardship thus caused was only partially alleviated by government and private aid to the poor. The distribution of such aid evinced a clear awareness on the part of its donors of the dangers to public order posed by a situation in which the reactions of the urban poor remained generally similar to those of the small market towns and countryside – inchoate protest against individuals and conditions over which no control could be exerted, rather than organized action – which did not often appear possible in a situation of continual and massive price fluctuations – in defence of wages or employment.

This situation was changing. The amplitude of price fluctuations had already been substantially reduced by the eighteenth-century programmes of road building; but only the establishment of a railway network would make possible a decisive break with the economy, society and social psychology of the Ancien Régime.

Until this occurred the typical French worker would be the artisan working in a small workshop rather than the factory worker. This was true in Paris, for example, where the majority found work in industries catering for the material needs of the population – food, clothing, furniture and housing – or in the typically Parisian luxury industries, all traditionally operating on a small scale.

Paris was the centre of administration, trade, finance and communication. Because of its concentration of population and of wealth, it tended to be too expensive for entrepreneurs to establish large workshops and factories, since they were unwilling or unable to pay more than they would elsewhere for sites, rents and wages. Although the presence there of skilled labour attracted some new industry – engineering, for example – Paris primarily served as the distribution centre for goods produced elsewhere and, of course, on account of its large population it provided the largest market both for consumer goods and for high-quality luxury goods. The economist Lavollée, writing as late as 1865, observed that 'what above all else characterizes Parisian industry is the extreme division of labour, the variety and small scale. Large factories are few and far between, small workshops are very numerous; there is nothing to resemble the character of factory towns where several large factories each employ hundreds and thousands of workers at the same work.' Links between workshop owners, merchants and those employed were often intimate. Conflicts of interest obviously existed between employer and wage-earner but, in a situation in which the latter could often hope one day to set himself up in a small business, a certain common outlook tended to limit the development of a separate consciousness on the part of the one or the other. The most important single employer of industrial labour in France was the textile industry. In towns like Mulhouse and Lille, for example, the most advanced techniques and forms of organization existed side by side with small-scale

'The real capital, here it is' by Moynet: the pride of the craftsman in his skill and the demand that his value to society be recognized.

production, the latter organized on the principle of 'putting out' work to workers in the surrounding countryside, a competitive system because of its low labour costs. The 'proletarian', in the broad Marxist sense of a factory wage-worker, existed then in only a few, isolated centres, and 1848 in France was not at any point a proletarian Revolution. But if this was not yet an industrial society, it was evidently in the process of becoming one.

By 1848 there coexisted three types of industrial production, one based on the factory, another on the artisan workshop, and a third on dispersed rural activity. This coexistence was made possible by the isolation and juxtaposition of, rather than competition between, regional economies.

Industrial development was indicated by technical innovation and above all by the growing use of coal as motive force for steam engines and as fuel for a new metallurgy. The number of stationary steam engines increased from 625 at the end of 1830 to 4,853 in 1847. But until the creation of a railway network, the cost of transporting coal from the dispersed coal basins limited this development. The use of waterwheels to generate hydraulic power was widespread. In textiles, although the increasing competition and decline of the more archaic forms of production were evident in the 1840s, thanks to the improvement of roads and waterways, high transport costs still served in most regions as an effective form of protection to the less efficient.

By comparison with British industry, that of France remained under-developed, though with isolated poles of growth – relatively dynamic regions and units that would, with cheaper transport, subsequently be given the opportunity to extend their markets and to enforce a more general modernization of the economy through the diffusion of new techniques and the weeding-out of archaic elements. The rapid development of transport and banking networks from the early years of the Second Empire would be decisive in stimulating this structural change, but even earlier its impulse added to the stresses existing within an essentially pre-industrial economy. Thus the economic crisis of 1847–48 was in many respects the crisis of a transition economy, of a society in process of modernization. The situation contained elements typical of both old and new regimes, which greatly adds to the complexity of any explanation of subsequent events.

New large-scale mechanized enterprises were being created. In sub-stantial parts of artisan manufacture, effective control of production was passing to the merchants who organized sales and controlled credit. Workers in artisan trades – even the master artisans who employed them – as well as factory workers, were more and more conscious of external forces encroaching on their lives, all seeking to make them more efficient at lower cost. These new forces were identified as those of 'capitalism' or of 'financial feudalism'.

The contrast in the living standards of rich and poor that daily greeted the eyes of the urban populations, especially in the larger towns, was often extreme. For as long as such a contrast was felt to be inevitable, it could be accepted only with resignation, or with a resentment that might burst out in violence. But new ideas and the diffusion of a more critical outlook were bound to erode this attitude, were bound to widen the concept of resistance to exploitation – a resistance already evident in the case of workers defending their professional interests by striking.

The literate were obviously the most receptive to new ideas, and their number was rapidly increasing. This was especially true where skilled workers built upon, rather than forgot, their elementary education whose usefulness was proved to them in their daily work. In the larger cities, above all in Paris, their constant contacts with members of the lower middle classes, declassed intellectuals and workers generated an intellectual atmosphere in which they thrived. Less or more than a proletariat, these strata together constituted the 'people'. Their social and political conscious-ness was not entirely the product of poor material conditions: it stemmed also from the awareness of, from the access to, ideas, and from the desire to act – all of which were consequences of the relatively privileged position of the skilled worker, who was sheltered from the extreme degradation and intellectually destructive effects of factory life and of unskilled manual labour.

DEUX UTOPIES.

I

UNE RUE DE PARIS.

II.

UN DÉSERT ENTRE LA CALIFORNIE ET LE TEXAS.

'Two utopias'. Hostile comment on the dreams of socialist thinkers and in particular on Cabet's efforts to establish an ideal society.

Republican and socialist newspapers and pamphlets, which stressed the need for representative government as a means of ending economic insecurity and misery, proved increasingly attractive as the more prosperous earlier years of the decade 1840–50 gave way to a period of intense crisis. A revolutionary consciousness was evolving, but only where resentment of exploitation could combine with the formulation of alternatives. This was part of the significance of Paris as a political centre. From Paris ideas were transmitted to towns and villages throughout France through the press, migrant workers, and idealistic, ambitious or alienated individuals drawn from a variety of social groups. Here large sections of the population might be mobilized against the existing authorities with revolutionary consequences for the whole of France.

In an outpouring of writings and ideas, ineffectively controlled by the administration, hostility toward the rich was increasingly combined with aspirations for greater economic security and for human dignity, an attitude embodied, for instance, in the newspaper *L'Atelier*, written by artisans. Men who would become political activists during the Second Republic (1848–51) wanted justice, wanted to assume a place in society, wanted their value as the producers of all society's goods to be fully recognized. The bitter opposition to the more extreme forms of economic exploitation, the desire to establish mutual aid associations and producers' co-operatives, even the attractiveness of the utopian ideals of men such as Etienne Cabet were all aspects of this desire for recognition, for status, for a measure of equality.

The political ideology of the Left throughout the Second Republic, for all that it was to contain frequent references to class conflict, would retain much that was vague and idealistic. Even the June days of 1848 were not to destroy the ideal of the coexistence of rich and poor. But more practical demands were also to emerge, demands involving taxation of the wealthy to provide both material aid and means for the satisfaction of the social aspirations of the less well off. Cheap credit and better educational opportunities, it was said, should combine with universal suffrage to enable all to participate in the political process, and through it in the control of their own destinies. Reform was visualized as a gradual pacific process, and this made possible the collaboration of democrats and socialists; but the prospect of any kind of reduction in their privileged situation was enough to frighten conservatives of all political hues, who constantly characterized the proponents of reform as 'communists' and social levellers. Their fears were intensified by a widespread literature which, in describing the 'social problem', tended to identify the labouring poor with those elements on the fringe of criminality that are to be found in any large city. Their identification of poverty with criminality was encouraged in this period, since, with limited economic development restricting employment opportunities, many were forced in desperation into morally or legally doubtful activities. The wealthy saw the urban poor as barbarians within the gates, awaiting an opportunity to avenge their misery in a holocaust of murder, destruction and looting. Poverty itself, and their own contrasting existence, they justified as the consequences of, respectively, moral and intellectual weakness and of strength. It followed that their society was not at fault: if misery existed this was the fault of the miserable, their sufferings being God's punishment for their inherent wickedness.

The historian A. J. Tudesq described France in the period of constitutional monarchy (1815–48) as being in transition from a relatively rigid, hierarchical society of orders to a more fluid capitalist society founded on wealth from industry. Those who possessed power were those who possessed wealth, either in the form of land, the most common form of wealth in most regions, or in the form of manufacturing, commercial and financial enterprises. Social and political power was based on economic power.

Their economic roles gave men prestige and influence as landlords, and creditors. Moreover – and the point is worth stressing – this was an age when the geographical and intellectual horizons of most people were limited by their total or functional illiteracy and by their inability to travel, so that their capacity to pose an alternative to the social *status quo* was necessarily also limited. Only wealth could purchase the education necessary to form a critical intelligence. As a result, the dominance of the wealthy, if often bitterly resented, was not generally exposed to a sustained challenge.

The Revolution of 1830 had threatened the monopoly of power by the wealthy, but only in the major cities where skilled, literate artisans were politicized through contact with a middle-class milieu. In Paris the masses had played a major part in overthrowing the regime. There and elsewhere *liberté* had been proclaimed, and had been taken to mean the freedom to express discontent in all its forms. Repression had soon ended disorder. A political compromise had extended the electorate, but not beyond the ranks of 'responsible', property-owning men. Fear of disorder created a fundamental community of interest within the élite, among the Notables, as it was again to do after the 1848 Revolution. Whatever their ideological or economic differences – Orléanists and Legitimists, landowners and businessmen – all would support the defence of social order: and thanks to the monopoly of the public office they enjoyed as a corollary of their education, they would be able efficiently to control society through the civil administration, the judiciary and the army. Electoral campaigns, with small numbers of voters subject to personal influences, would centre on material interests rather than ideology. The men elected were those whose superior wealth, culture and presumed connections in Paris made them most likely usefully to serve local interests. The world of politics, administration and finance was dominated by a narrow circle, sharing similar interests and working together to develop these. Power in these spheres was centred in Paris, which explains the political significance of the city. Control of the capital was likely to ensure predominance throughout France. There were no alternative centres of authority.

The *grands Notables* – landowners, financiers, major industrialists, but also politicians and administrators – collaborated in extending their economic power and safeguarding their social and political authority. This was a group given unity not simply by shared material interests, but by an entire style of life. It was a style made possible by wealth – wealth that afforded them similar education, provided the leisure to make participation in public life possible, and allowed them to enjoy dual residence (a house in town and an estate in the country). Their outlook was dominated more by their attachment to the land, and the supposed values of rural society, than by their seasonal residence in Paris or other large cities. Although political power was exerted from the city, the politicians' conceptualization of French society – and hence their objectives – was heavily influenced by the fundamental outlook of the landowner.

The wealth of this social group was symbolized in the public mind by men like James de Rothschild. The group's dominance, acceptable in times of prosperity, became less supportable with the decline of prosperity. Then the inevitable imposition of restrictions on credit (determined by the regents of the Bank of France, who were themselves members of the dominant group), whose effects were felt throughout the economy, would worsen the existing crisis, and threaten the economic survival of a mass of small businessmen. Thus there would be the alienation from the regime of much of the urban middle class, who blamed government and financiers for hard times. In such a situation the normal alliance of property-owners might disintegrate, and along with alienation might develop a growing attraction to the vague, essentially moderate and humanitarian ideals of Republicanism, to something other than the cold materialism which now constituted a threat, and to something which also, through the promise of an extended suffrage, offered participation in the decision-making process, in an effort to control economic forces in their own interests. In this way, in 1847–48 the normal parliamentary and local struggles among the Notables, struggles between 'ins' and 'outs', and for office and patronage, grew into a more general discussion of constitutional principles, including the role of the monarch in government and the extension of the franchise.

The February Revolution was preceded, and in part caused, by a social crisis that had begun some years earlier – a crisis of a familiar type, spreading from agriculture to commerce and industry. There was a sharp rise in the price of grain. Thus on the market at Caen, for example, the price of a hectolitre of wheat rose from frs 22·89 in 1846 to a peak of frs 49·26 in May of 1847. The economic situation was worsened, however, by the effects of a new type of economic crisis caused by international financial speculation, a shortage of credit facilities and industrial overproduction. The elements of the old and new crisis combined to cause a decline in revenue of all kinds.

Although a recovery was evident following a good harvest in 1847, prices and unemployment remained high. The Revolution of February 1848 was thus in large part due to the social unrest caused by this economic crisis.

Discontent in all sections of the population had deprived Louis-Philippe's government of many of its usual supporters, and there was anyway a lack of confidence in a regime that was pursuing what appeared to be a weak foreign policy and that was embarrassed by scandals in high places. This discontent had accelerated and served to radicalize a campaign for suffrage reform. When on 22 February demonstrators clashed with the military in Paris, the deaths that occurred stimulated a full-scale insurrection. The king and his ministers seem to have suffered a crisis of confidence and the administration collapsed. In the absence of determined leadership, and given the government's failure to act to preserve order, there was nothing to impede the seizure of power by a small group of Republicans in Paris. Republicanism was the only political faith that appealed to the crowds in the streets of the city, who supported the assumption of power by its best-known representatives. These were mainly journalists associated with two newspapers, the moderate Le National and the more radical La Réforme. Also included were the social reformer Louis Blanc, and the man known

23 February; the consequences of a clash between demonstrators and the army on the Boulevard des Capucines. Political compromise instead of Revolution was thus made impossible.

as Albert, a worker long involved in secret societies. The heterogeneity of this government by popular demand was to be a source of weakness and division, but a certain unity existed in so far as the majority of its members, though politically Republican, were socially conservative. These, who had most of them been opposition deputies during the July monarchy, assumed control of the most important ministries: Alphonse de Lamartine was at foreign affairs, Adolphe Crémieux at justice, Pierre Marie at public works, Louis Garnier-Pagès at finance and Armand Marrast was mayor of Paris. At the key ministry of the interior, Alexandre Ledru-Rollin would show sympathy toward aspiration for social change but, in the last resort, he would be motivated by his fear of the Paris mob and of violent revolution.

Provincial opinion must have thought this Revolution profoundly Parisian and very sudden. Only in Paris and, to a lesser extent, in Lyon, Limoges and Rouen, did the totality of the economic and political factors combine to create a revolutionary situation. Elsewhere the Revolution must have presented a somewhat artificial and imposed character. Conservatives accepted it because of its apparently moderate intentions and because there was no agreed alternative.

The throne-room at the Tuileries palace, 24 February 1848.

Above, 'The Parliament of Labour', detail of an engraving by Wattier and Riffaut. Initially the establishment of the Luxembourg Commission seemed to promise representation of the interests of workers.

Below, the Provisional Government: from right to left, Arago, Ledru-Rollin, Dupont de l'Eure, Marie, Lamartine; standing right to left, Louis Blanc, Flocon, Crémieux, Marrast, Albert, Garnier-Pagès.

National workshop for tailors, established in the prison of Clichy, Paris.

The early measures introduced by the men who were now the provisional government of the Republic evinced a great concern for legality, order and administrative continuity. For many, indeed, moderation such as these measures displayed seemed assured by the presence in the government of the aristocratic poet Lamartine.

Popular pressure nevertheless forced the new government to introduce measures which, in the context of the period, were radical: universal male suffrage, a reduction by one hour of the working day, national workshops as part of a guaranteed right to work, and the Luxembourg commission to inquire into further possible social reforms. The second of these measures, however, was ineffective, the third was merely an expedient to provide essential relief to the unemployed and clear them off the streets, and the fourth was a means of postponing necessary reform. Besides, in recognizing the debts of the Orléanist monarchy, in supporting the Bank of France in its financial difficulties and in a number of other measures designed to maintain financial stability and re-establish business confidence, the government revealed its commitment to support the existing social order.

The workers in Paris and in many provincial centres looked forward to a new era of social harmony and a better life. They were concerned to affirm their dignity as workers, and, through the organizations in which they participated – the mutual aid societies, professional associations, national workshop units, and the Comité central des ouvriers du département de la Seine, which grouped the delegates of the various corporations elected to the Luxembourg commission – would maintain pressure on the government to ensure that reforms were made. In the more middle-class clubs, and in the mass of newspapers that appeared, the great themes were those of the 1789 Revolution and especially a variety of interpretations of Robespierre's 'Declaration of the Rights of Man', reinterpreted to include the right to work.

This activity contributed to the development of a popular political consciousness, to continuing agitation, and also to the heightening of Conservative fears of further revolution. Conservatives supported the provisional government as a bulwark against this and as a defence against a wave of popular disturbances that followed the Revolution, when workers and peasants interpreted *liberté* as the right to remove whatever they disliked. The events so precipitated – machine-breaking, assaults on foreign workers, strikes, threats against employers and money-lenders, depredations in the state and private forests in support of customary rights of usage

One of the many political clubs whose activities helped to maintain agitation.

17 March 1848. For Conservatives, this was a frightening display of the potential for mass action.

and widespread refusals to pay taxes – promoted a desire for strong, authoritative government.

This was reinforced by attempts in Paris to push the government in a revolutionary direction. The first great demonstration occurred on 17 March in support of a demand for postponement of the elections of a constituent assembly and national guard officers so as to give more time for radical propaganda. This and subsequent displays on 16 April and 15 May strengthened Conservative desire for reaction.

For many, even of the poor, the Republic existed as a broken promise. Economic crisis continued and was worsened by the lack of confidence due to the political situation. Unpopular taxes continued to be collected and, worse, a supplementary tax of 45 per cent was imposed on land, increasing the disaffection of the peasantry. Those who bought and sold, or who had property, became increasingly critical of a government that seemed to do nothing to improve their situation but instead pandered to the workers of Paris, who, it was said, in the national workshops did nothing and yet were paid at the nation's expense.

By mid-March, it is evident from a reading of press, Conservatives had got over the initial shock of revolution, and a broad Conservative alliance was evolving. The majority of peasants, and of provincial workers and tradesmen expecting nothing from the government, saw no alternative (bar apathy) to following the lead of the traditional ruling élites.

The campaign preceding the general election of 23 April was the first to be fought for the allegiance of a mass electorate. In the absence of organized parties, candidates selected themselves or were selected by small groups. The Conservative campaign was based on a call for the defence of order, of property, of the family and religion. It attacked the new forty-five-centime tax and the tyranny of Paris. Almost everyone expressed loyalty to the Republic, and made some vague commitment to improving conditions for the poor. Promises of radical social transformation were generally lacking. Given the fact that this government, on ideological grounds, opposed electoral manipulation, the only opposition to the traditional Notables, and to Conservatives more generally, came from the more radical Republicans. But in a situation in which men voted for those whose names they knew, or for those who were recommended to them by men whose advice they respected, usually on the basis of their wealth or superior knowledge (especially religious), radical influence was limited. Pressure rarely needed to be exerted by the Notables, but obviously it could be. Most peasants and workers voted as though in recognition of their inferior status.

The constituent assembly met on 4 May. It was bound to be dominated by Conservatives, whether Republican or Monarchist. Of 880 deputies, perhaps 100 were radicals. Most deputies were relatively wealthy representatives of the bourgeois professions, provincials with little sympathy for Paris or her particular problems. They were politically inexperienced and thus susceptible to manipulation by experienced parliamentarians. The support of this assembly strengthened the government's determination to resist the pressure constantly applied by the Parisian mob, by whom the election would very soon be seen as a victory for reaction.

The election by the assembly of an executive commission to replace the provisional government immediately revealed its conservatism by excluding the prominent radicals Blanc and Albert. At the same time, the brutal repression of a demonstration in Rouen, protesting the election results there, created a feeling on the Left that a plot was afoot, and that these deputies, in denying the Revolution, were betraying their confidence.

All shades of opinion in the press, and speeches in the clubs, from this time point to a growing feeling that an armed clash was inevitable. In this political conflict, the national workshops stood as a symbol of the Revolution and of its hopes for workers and the most radical Republicans; for Conservatives, on the other hand, it symbolized the socialist threat.

Above, *15 May 1848: the Assembly invaded by demonstrators.*

Left, *Barbès, speaking at the Assembly, demands help for Poland.*

The reality of this threat was confirmed when on 15 May a mob invaded the assembly demanding French support for a Polish revolt against the Russians. Some leaders of the revolutionary clubs seized the opportunity to attempt a *coup* – an attempt doomed to rapid failure because of the absence of agreement or adequate organization on the Left. For the first time a large number of workers from the national workshops participated in a demonstration, confirming the increasing belief that they constituted the Revolution organized.

The government adopted a more and more repressive policy toward the press and the clubs. The national guard in Paris was purged, the most authoritative leaders on the Left, men like Armand Barbès and Auguste Blanqui were arrested. Conservatives continued to press for more determined action and combined with Republicans of *Le National* and *La Réforme* – those radicals associated with Ledru-Rollin – to condemn the demonstration of 15 May as an intolerable assault on the rights of the democratically elected representatives of the nation.

In response to the exaggerated conservatism of many deputies, for some time in June the executive commission and its government reaffirmed its republicanism, promising reforms of the tax structure and the nationalization of railway and assurance companies. Faced by the Conservative outburst that this precipitated, the government, unwilling to risk political isolation, capitulated and finally decided to dissolve the national workshops.

In the meantime, workers in Paris, dissatisfied with the government, suffering from unemployment, seeing the workshops as an essential source of income and the only concrete gain of the Revolution they had fought for in February, became increasingly susceptible to extremists, who included – significantly – a variety of Bonapartist agitators.

II

On 21 June a decree ordered the expulsion of all unmarried workers from the national workshops. This was in addition to existing restrictions on entry and to plans for the movement of workers to public works in the provinces. The decree, presented in a hasty, incompetent manner, totally failed to publicize the alternative forms of relief that it had been decided to implement.

This was the immediate cause of the June insurrection. The official inquiry into its causes would describe it as an organized socialist revolt; Marx would create another myth – of 'how the workers, without leaders, without a common plan, without means and, for the most part, lacking weapons held in check for five days' the army and the national guard. Truth lies somewhere in between.

Most of those arrested claimed, under interrogation, that they had been forced to take part. No doubt many were, but by the excitement of the moment, or out of fear of criticism by their neighbours rather than because of overt threats. As in February, this must have seemed a just insurrection, and one quite as likely to succeed. The impending dissolution of the national workshops threatened to bring with it not only unemployment but a future without hope. The insurgents, or at least those interrogated, evinced a confused socio-political imagery, dominated not by socialist ideas but by the old hatred of the rich, a hatred reinforced by the disappointment following upon February. They still demanded not social revolution so much as reforms that would bring them increased material comfort and dignity.

This was a revolt of the poorer elements of the Parisian population, of the 'people', of those most adversely affected by economic crisis – some of the small shopkeepers, tavern-keepers and owners of workshops but primarily of the artisans and labourers. Given the structure of Parisian industry, it included relatively few factory workers. Numerically the most dispossessed, however, the workers of all kinds predominated, particularly those of the building trades, metal and engineering workers, those producing shoes, clothing and furniture and the unskilled of all industries.

Anything between fifteen and fifty thousand people were involved, inhabitants of the eastern part of Paris, of the poorest quarters: St Jacques, St Marcel and St Antoine. To a significant degree it was a spontaneous insurrection, the most prominent leaders of the Left having been arrested after 15 May. A certain basic unity was conferred on the movement by shared ideas and slogans, and by a grassroots leadership that emerged as the conflict developed, notably out of the existing neighbourhood organization provided by the national guard and national workshops.

Other than the defence of their own quarters, the insurgents appear to have had limited military aims. The army had already taken the decision to concentrate and so to crush any further insurrection, avoiding the fatal dispersal of its forces that had occurred in February. This cautious tactic allowed the insurrection to develop to such an extent that only bitter fighting could end it. In this repression the guard mobile, organized from unemployed youths, and national guards participated – the latter being more likely to intervene depending on the middle-class composition of any given unit. Many workers also joined in this repression, often in defence of a Republic they believed to be threatened by extremists, even by partisans of monarchy. The question of who participated in the repression is thus a complex one to answer.

This insurrection of 23–26 June and its defeat fatally weakened the Republic by separating the moderate Republicans – the only republicans

A popular engraving portraying the insurrection of June 1848, suppressed by General Cavaignac.

most of France could accept in power – from the workers, who alone at this time might have provided mass support for Republican institutions. Even the more radical Republicans, typified by Ledru-Rollin, had been frightened by the Parisian mob and were passive during the insurrection, stressing the point that social reform must be gradual and the product of an agreed compromise with vested interests, not of a recourse to violence.

At news of the insurrection in Paris, national guards throughout the provinces had organized themselves to rush to the defence of order – a 'sacred union against anarchy' had been created, led by those with most prestige and influence. In the constituent assembly itself, Conservatives of all political groups had conferred on Cavaignac, the minister of war, supreme power for the emergency, revealing a willingness to accept the dictatorship of a general even before that of Louis-Napoléon. The survival of their society was at stake!

Karl Marx believed that June saw 'the first great battle between the two classes that split modern society'. Sociologically speaking this was an over simplification, but it reflected a contemporary feeling that 'The class war was declared' (Rémusat). Social hatreds had been intensified and, even after victory, Conservatives were pessimistic about the future of France. They presumed that if the insurrection in Paris had succeeded it would have spread through France. They saw it as only one part of a massive, nation-wide conspiracy to destroy them.

III

In gratitude for the June victory the assembly retained Cavaignac at the head of the government. But gratitude faded rapidly as the Conservative reaction in the country gathered pace. In local elections in July, August and September social power was retained by the traditional Notables, and there was evidence of a growing will to use it.

The new constitution that emerged from the assembly also revealed the more intense conservatism of this body, especially when compared with drafts prepared before June. It did little more than pay lip-service to Republican ideals. Of great significance for the immediate future was its provision for the election of a president – one who would control the executive machinery of government – by universal suffrage.

Conservatives everywhere reiterated their demands for further repression; their continued lack of confidence was symptomatic of a more general malaise caused, in large part, by a renewed crisis in agriculture due to the overproduction of wheat and wine, resulting in a glut on many markets and declining prices. This again restricted rural purchasing power, and also the degree to which commercial and industrial recovery could occur; but for the towns it at least had the merit of sharply reducing the cost of living.

In the countryside, even those small producers who were engaged in subsistence farming needed to sell something in order to raise cash to pay taxes, or the interest on loans. They found this increasingly difficult to do, and resistance to tax collectors became the most common sign of mass discontent.

Repression increasingly drove radicals underground and led to the formation of secret societies. The importance of these was exaggerated by both government and the Conservative press, increasing the fears of those who read the latter, but encouraging those who wanted social change. A polarization of political forces had occurred. Most moderate Republicans were discouraged by events. They felt betrayed by the masses who had proved themselves to be too impatient and demanding, and easily led astray by demagogues. They tended either to retire from politics or to support the defence of order (or, in a minority of cases, to align themselves with the radicals associated with Ledru-Rollin in defence of Republican institutions).

These radicals, the parliamentary Montagne (so called by analogy with the radical segment of the National Convention of 1792–93, which had been nicknamed 'the Mountain' because its members occupied the highest rows of seats in the building), increasingly attracted support by their vigorous resistance to Conservative proposals for more intensive repression. Their betrayal of the insurgents in June was in part forgotten. Repression forced a broad alliance on the Left, first seen in an electoral alliance in

Portrait of General Cavaignac,
by Ary Scheffer.

September 1848, and in the organization of a group called Solidarité
républicaine in November, designed to link radical groups throughout
France. The propaganda of the Left became manifestly less doctrinaire,
and tended to base itself on simple appeals to basic interests, particularly the
right to work for the urban workers, and cheap credit to democratize
property ownership in the countryside. Peasant discontent, especially in
the Midi and above all in the south-east where there was most resistance to
tax collection, created an audience willing to listen.

Another, and more significant, dynamic element in political life during
this second half of 1848 was the rise of Louis-Napoléon Bonaparte, a
nephew of the emperor. The legend of the latter had been created by
substantial literary activity and by the tales of veterans of the Imperial
armies. The empire was remembered by most peasants as a period of
prosperity. Glory had an appeal above the dullness of everyday life. From
the spring of 1848 there had been a flourishing of Bonapartist journals
using the various aspects of the Napoléon legend to appeal to all social
groups. Its effectiveness had been demonstrated by the success of Louis-
Napoléon in two parliamentary election campaigns. As a candidate for the
presidency this man had two great assets in his name and in his previous
non-involvement in the politics of the Republic; both stood him in good
stead in competition with political figures whose names were less familiar
to the masses, or, if known, were as likely to arouse antipathy as sympathy.

By the end of October Conservative political leaders were forced to
take Louis-Napoléon seriously because of his evident popularity. Many
would have preferred Cavaignac, who had at least proved himself in
defending order, but it became obvious that he would not succeed. To
Conservative leaders like Thiers, Louis-Napoléon seemed a libertine and a
fool, and he in turn seems deliberately to have cultivated their belief that
they could control him.

Far left, *designed to celebrate the return of the remains of Napoleon to France, this was one of many engravings which served to establish the Napoleonic legend.*

Left, *how should one vote in the presidential election? Why, for Louis-Napoléon whose name at least is familiar!*

Below, *Louis-Napoléon, 1848, by Daumier. The nephew, pulled along by a bedraggled imperial eagle, is kept afloat by his great uncle's hat.*

The judgment of Paris. The presidential candidates: Louis-Napoléon, Cavaignac, Lamartine, Thiers, Ledru-Rollin.

The election of December 1848 resulted in an overwhelming victory for Louis-Napoléon, with 5,434,226 votes compared with 1,448,107 for Cavaignac, 370,119 for Ledru-Rollin and 36.920 for Raspail. Even among workers in Paris and Lyon there was substantial support for Bonaparte, and not simply in revulsion against Cavaignac, the 'butcher of June', but as proof positive that they were willing to accept the dictatorship of a great man when that of a social class was becoming intolerable. He seemed to promise, if not liberty, reform and greater equality, which the more politically minded ardently desired.

Conservatives interpreted the victory of Louis-Napoléon as a victory for Conservative principles. The composition of his first government seemed to bear out their view. It was a coalition of Orléanists, Legitimists and one Republican, and it was led by Odilon Barrot, the last chief minister of Louis-Philippe.

Under this government, Republican officials were purged at all levels, and a campaign against the assembly, calling for its dissolution, was encouraged. It was desired that a new, more conservative body be elected to produce the organic laws that would implement the constitution. On 29 January 1849 the assembly voted its own dissolution: it had become convinced of its ineffectiveness in a situation in which the government ignored parliamentary defeats and was supported by a declaration of the president that ministers were responsible to him and not to it – this last being a significant step in the move toward personal government, though its significance was ignored by Conservative parliamentarians since, for the moment, it served their purposes. New elections were to be held on 13 May and, in the campaign that preceded them, the process of assimilating Orléanist liberalism and Legitimist authoritarianism into a gospel of order was strikingly evident. It was said that, in a social order established by God, wealth was the reward for ability and hard work, and that the only antidotes to the human greed and laziness that produced socialism were the Church and the army.

More than ever the moderate Republicans seemed to have lost all initiative. The only resistance to Conservative and governmental pressures came from the alliance of radicals and socialists, which organized support for candidates accepting their principles through committees in Paris and other major centres, and which gave advice and aid to a loosely structured organization of local committees. This '*démo-soc*' propaganda promised recognition of the right to work, legislation limiting working hours, nationalization of the railways, canals, mines, insurance companies and banks, progressive taxation and protection for small property-owners, tradesmen and peasants against 'financial feudalism'.

The campaign and constant police interference with radical propaganda helped maintain a continuous agitation within society and so generated numerous incidents – all of which contributed to a heightening of the political consciousness.

In the new assembly sat 75–80 moderate Republicans, about 500 other Conservatives (including approximately 200 Legitimists), and about 180 radical Republicans and socialists, with a more committed core of about 130. It has been estimated that *démo-soc* candidates obtained 2,357,000 votes (23·7 per cent of those eligible to vote, but 34·8 per cent of the votes cast), moderate Republicans only 800,000 votes.

Not only a political but a social polarization was evident in these election results between the *grands Notables* sitting on the Right in the new assembly and the lower middle-class elements on the Left, with a virtual elimination of the middle middle-class elements typical of moderate Republicanism. Socially the Conservative majority was far more cohesive, and this cohesiveness was an element of political strength.

In most areas the election was taken as further confirmation of the power of the Notables, particularly in the north, north-east and west, but the extent of support for *démo-soc* candidates came as a great surprise. It indicated the existence of a 'Red France', in the centre, west and north of the Massif Central; in the valleys of the Saône and Rhône and neighbouring areas; in Alsace; and in the departments bordering the Mediterranean – the Midi, Acquitaine, and Pyrenees, where *démo-soc* candidates gained 30 per cent of the votes. Support for them was especially evident in urban centres: more generally, it seems that the more concentrated the population, the more likely this support. For such support to be generated it was essential that middle-class elements, relatively well educated and open to new ideas, should live in close contact with peasants, artisans and workers to serve as a transmission belt for ideas from outside the town or village. The poor central, eastern and southern agricultural regions were characterized by a large proportion of peasant landowners thus enjoying a degree of independence, and a concentrated habitat permitting awareness of common interests.

This success by the *démo-socs* – for such it appeared to be – intensified Conservative pessimism and encouraged demands for restriction of the suffrage and for stronger government. To the *démo-socs* it gave an exaggerated sense of their own importance.

IV

A French military expedition had been dispatched to Italy with the intention of preventing Austrian intervention in support of the Pope, who had met with revolution in his temporal kingdom. It became increasingly evident that the purpose of the expedition was not only to limit the growth of the Austrian sphere of influence, but was also intended to restore to the Pope his domains, presumably in order to increase Roman Catholic support for Louis-Napoléon.

The Montagne in the assembly bitterly opposed the assault on the Roman Republic, and called for a rising in protest against unconstitutional action. But it did no more than participate in a half-hearted and pacific demonstration in Paris on 13 June 1849. This attracted between perhaps six and eight thousand participants. In a Paris wracked by cholera, and vividly remembering the repression of the previous June, little enthusiasm could be expected. The demonstration was easily dispersed, its leaders imprisoned or, like Ledru-Rollin, forced into exile. Most members of the Montagne denied any responsibility.

The government reaction was a new wave of repression. Conservatives more generally were alarmed by reports of preparations for an uprising in the Midi, and by the development of organizations like Solidarité républicaine. On 10 March 1850, in spite of intense governmental activity, Republicans were victorious in twenty-one of the thirty-one elections needed to replace deputies arrested after 13 June.

As part of the ever-increasing repression, a new education law was introduced in March 1850. It was evidently intended – by encouraging the Church to extend its network of schools, and the parish priest in each commune to exercise surveillance over the lay schoolteacher – to discipline the masses. The Church, after its experience of revolution, was anxious to

Above, *events of 13 June 1849: action against the left-wing press. National Guards smash machinery at Boulé's the printers.*

Below left, *1850 political repression. Cartoon showing a woman being arrested for wearing a* Red *shawl.*

Below right, *the new electoral law of 31 May 1850 took the vote away from nearly three million voters, chiefly workers who changed domicile in search of jobs. Cham's cartoon portrays the supposed anomaly by which judge and criminal, itinerants both, find themselves disenfranchized.*

Atteinte et convaincue de porter un châle rouge.

72.CHAM

use Holy Scripture and its own organizational resources for socio-political purposes.

On 28 April further electoral setbacks confirmed the Conservative belief that universal suffrage was an element of instability. The massive victory of Louis-Napoléon in the presidential elections had given them an initial confidence in their ability to influence the electorate; but, increasingly, they viewed the prospect of the next general and presidential elections, due in 1852, with dismay. So on 31 May 1850 a new electoral law took effect, introducing a three-year residential qualification for voting, in place of the existing six-month period. This and the complexities of the registration procedure disenfranchised 2,809,000 men, mainly workers: 62 per cent of the electorate was excluded in Paris, 51 per cent in the Nord, 43 per cent in the Loire and the Seine Inférieure, 40 per cent in the Rhône (all relatively industrialized areas – the figure was only 11 per cent in the more agricultural Meuse).

It was observed at the time that Louis-Napoléon and the ministers appointed by him avoided all identification with this electoral law, leaving the parliamentary processes to leaders in the assembly.

There, and in the country generally, if a Conservative alliance of convenience continued to exist, its members were patently unable to solve the problems of France themselves. Conservatives were consequently more and more drawn into accepting a Bonapartist solution. Contempt was everywhere evident for parliamentary institutions as conducive to indecision and weakness. If, initially, Louis-Napoléon had appeared to subordinate himself to the Barrot ministry and to the assembly, he increasingly selected ministers who were dependent on himself; and, through provincial tours and press campaigns, he created an image of himself as a man capable of restoring prosperity but frustrated by the squabbling and self-seeking politicians in the assembly.

As early as the end of 1849, Conservative politicians had become aware of the threat to their political power posed by a new Caesarism. Most *démo-soc* politicians were more optimistic. They professed to believe that a legal course of action would bring electoral victory in 1852. They claimed to be protected from any attempt at a preventive *coup d'état* by the president by the support they commanded among the people and in the army. They thus refused to be provoked by legislation such as the electoral law.

A certain amount of criticism was levelled at these passive tactics, especially by exiles safe in London, but also by a minority of deputies, adopting for themselves the title of 'New Mountain'. These, especially, engaged in more intense organizational activity, with the purpose of defending the constitution, and, for 1852, the organization of the disenfranchised to demand their right to vote, by force if necessary. The main centres of activity of this group were the Rhône region and the south-east, partly because of the high level of discontent in these areas, due to the economic situation, partly because of the enthusiasm of local leaders. A wave of arrests in October 1850 restored much of the influence of the more moderate leaders. This was part of a process in which the networks of underground organizations were constantly broken by police action, then reorganized. The links between secret societies in any one area were never more than tenuous, due to local and personal rivalries, while those between regions were even more difficult to maintain. There was suspicion in many quarters of the zeal of the Parisian deputies who provided co-ordination at regional and national levels, thanks to their failure to follow words with action on previous occasions, and this stimulated localism. Police repression and the existence of informers created a natural suspicion of contacts.

As 1852 approached, Conservative fears became more intense. Relations between the president and the conservative politicians in the assembly worsened under the pressure of competing ambitions. In January 1851 Louis-Napoléon dismissed General Changarnier, who was in command of the Paris area, and in whom Conservatives had had great confidence; the latter, although they regarded this as a provocation, were too fearful of provoking a political crisis to offer more than mild resistance. The divisions among Conservatives, particularly between Legitimists and Orléanists, left the political initiative to Louis-Napoléon. Many conservatives were willing to vote in favour of constitutional revision to permit the prince-president to retain his office for an indefinite period, but even this solution to the threat of political instability proved impossible, since constitutional revision required support of three-quarters of the deputies in the assembly. This failure left Louis-Napoléon with no alternative but to retire meekly in 1852, or to attempt a *coup*. The behaviour of Conservative deputies was indicative of the unwillingness of Conservatives generally to oppose his pretensions as long as they believed society to be faced by the threat of imminent socialist revolution. Given this basic desire for social order, no one would risk an initiative designed to resist Louis-Napoléon that might throw France into chaos.

Since the dismissal of the Barrot ministry in October 1849 senior administrative officials and army officers had been appointed on the basis of presumed loyalty to the president. For most army officers, the Bona-partist propaganda directed toward the army had little appeal. Their loyalties tended to be toward the monarchist pretenders, but, provided the right men could be placed at the summit of the military hierarchy to issue the necessary orders, the rest would obey. By the end of 1851 this organization was complete, and was symbolized by the presence of A. L. de Saint-Arnaud at the ministry of war.

V

On 2 December 1851 the *coup d'état* took place. In a proclamation, Louis-Napoléon appealed for support for the social order and the defence of the Republic, both supposedly threatened by the plots and obstructions of members of the assembly.

Most conservative political leaders in Paris had little enthusiasm for the *coup* but the resistance they offered was merely formal. Monarchist deputies, after gathering at the town hall of the 10th *arrondissement* and making a declaration of protest, seem to have vied with each other for the honour of undergoing imprisonment, of being proved to have done their duty, and, through imprisonment, to be absolved of all further responsibility in the affair. In having to make the difficult decision of whether or not to join Republicans and socialists in resisting a Conservative *coup*, what else could be expected of men frightened for the safety of society, which they believed to be under socialist attack? In the provinces reaction at first varied with the degree to which the reality of the Red menace was given credence, but insurrections in the south in resistance to the *coup* seemed to confirm the official view that the *démo-socs* had been preparing an insurrection for 1852 and that the *coup* was essentially a preventive measure. This in turn has been taken to confirm the need for Conservative unity. If many, and Legitimists in particular, suffered a bad conscience, Conservatives accepted the *coup* not in spite of the threat of dictatorship but because it was promised. Former liberals and moderate Republicans tended to support, or at least not oppose, government measures. Business groups wrote letters of congratulation; symptomatic of the attitudes of the wealthy, the 5 per cent *rente* (government stock) rose from 91·60 on 1 December to 100·90 on 16 December.

The Church would celebrate the victory of Louis-Napoléon with solemn *Te Deums*. The man who had restored the Pope was now destroying the menace of revolution. Once again the Church was closely allied with Conservative groups.

Most of the potential leaders of opposition were removed by preventive arrests. In Paris some *démo-soc* deputies formed a committee of resistance, but most workers seemed indifferent to the *coup*, which at least promised the restoration of universal suffrage. Louis-Napoléon still had much positive appeal. Armed resistance did occur on 4 December but attracted little support and was easily overcome. The defence of a Conservative assembly had little appeal.

Outside the capital the major cities were disturbed only by minor demonstrations. Militants were discouraged by obvious military preparedness and the news of the failure of resistance in Paris. The industrial towns in particular seem to have been indifferent, with workers, after years of economic crisis, making the best of a period of at least relative prosperity.

Right, 'Freedom to vote, 20–21 December 1851'. Propaganda print applauding the re-establishment of universal male suffrage and the plebiscite of 21 December 1851.

Above, people reading the proclamation of 2 December 1851 by the President of the Republic.

Below, death of Alphonse Baudin on a barricade in the Faubourg Saint-Antoine, 3 December 1851. This hitherto obscure deputy would in the closing years of the Second Empire serve as the symbol of the martyrdom of Republicans in 1851.

Over large areas there was armed resistance. The insurgents were primarily the peasants and artisans of the small towns and villages. There were three main areas in which large-scale uprisings occurred: in the centre, based in the Nièvre, and including the Allier and Cher and some cantons of the Yonne and Loire; in the south-west in the Gers, Lot-et-Garonne and Lot; and on the largest scale in the south-east, in the Drôme, Basses-Alpes and Var, extending into Languedoc, into the Ardèche, Gard, Hérault and Pyrénées-Orientales. Save for exceptions such as isolated cantons in the Sarthe, Jura and Saône-et-Loire, the populations to the north of a line following the middle and lower Loire did not rise.

Support was forthcoming for this insurrection for a variety of reasons. To those primarily lower middle-class elements and members of the liberal professions who had organized the underground societies and who now offered to lead resistance to the *coup*, a mixture of personal ambition and political ideals counted for much. They fought in defence of the Republic which, unsatisfactory though it was, might yet be reformed – a hope that Bonapartist dictatorship must end.

What was sufficient reason for middle-class intellectuals would not have attracted a mass following. Few rural artisans or peasants knew much about the constitution, and they cared less; few were hostile to Louis-Napoléon, but for years *démo-soc* propaganda had promised a transformation of society in their interests following on the elections set for 1852. Now the *coup* came as a threat to all these promises. Whereas after February 1848 the establishment of universal suffrage, of loosely organized political groups, and the principle of periodic elections had contributed to the institutionalization of protest against traditional grievance, this, the culminating act in the development of repression, seemed to close these channels of protest and call for a return to violent action. Now, after several years' experience of political agitation, protest assumed a more overtly political character. Rural artisans and peasants demanded the defence, not of the existing Republic but of that promised for 1852, with freedom from taxes and usurers, with land for all. The rich, the exploiters, were seeking to rob them of this. The risings came about from a sense of desperation, as part of a struggle for survival in unfavourable economic circumstances, their character being determined as much by local conditions and struggles for political influence as by national events. Sentiments of social hostility were everywhere evident, sentiments that were not so much ideologically based as part of an age-old hostility to the wealthy.

Artisans and tradesmen tended to be more politically aware than peasants. But they were nevertheless integrated into the rural community, and suffered with the rest of the poor from the reduction of income caused by a market glut and low agricultural prices after a series of good harvests.

Resistance to the *coup d'état* was a protest by the poor against the privileged – against those who employed them, who rented out land, who bought the land they hungered for, who loaned them money on usurious terms and speculated in the grains that were their daily bread. The poor protested mainly against increasing economic pressures but also from a feeling that their dignity as human beings had to be asserted.

In all this, political ideology had a limited part to play. Documents like Robespierre's 'Declaration of the Rights of Man' and the writings of a variety of socialists helped determine the shape and phraseology of the demands made, but the demands themselves were essentially based on the material needs of those involved. The motives of participants, where expressed, were generally confused. Most of them seem to have been unable to resist the apparent unanimity of the crowd. The majority of those arrested admitted to participating previously in a secret society, while often claiming to have been initially attracted by the friendly society activities which these adopted as a guise. Moreover, it had been rumoured that the whole of France had risen.

The insurrection was doomed to quick failure. Police repression allied with internal divisions, had weakened links between secret societies. The tendency had been toward localization, but preventive arrests and the failure of the larger towns to rise reinforced this, so that what occurred was a series of local, unco-ordinated risings in the countryside and small towns where military strength was insufficient to impose immediate repression. The scale of the uprisings in spite of these difficulties, however, reveals something of the discontent of the rural population; but this could not compensate for the lack of organization. In the face of regular troops the insurgents melted away, as did the first enthusiasm and the belief in a speedy, almost bloodless victory.

The areas of resistance to the *coup* included some of those troubled by agrarian disorders in previous years, in which population pressure on resources was intense, areas in which the ownership of small plots of land and patterns of village sociability gave a certain independence of mind and action to much of the population, and in which involvement in production for regional markets had broken down isolation.

In most areas peasants lacked such property and independence, lacked contact with new ideas of social organization, could not imagine a society differing from that in which they and their fathers lived, or relationships other than those of dependence and subservience. Most of the population either welcomed the *coup*, attracted by aspects of the Bonapartist legend, or at least accepted it, as they indifferently accepted everything done by the government, provided that they did not obviously lose by it.

A seal was set on the *coup* by a plebiscite, presenting, according to the government and Conservative press, a choice between order and anarchy.

Demolition of the building constructed in the courtyard of the Palais Bourbon to house the enlarged Assembly of 1848. A symbolic act.

Just as in 1848 Conservatives had accepted the provisional government as the best guarantee of order in the circumstances, so now they would accept Louis-Napoléon, sacrificing liberty if necessary for security.

There was government pressure on voters, especially in areas in which insurrections had occurred, but this did not cause – it merely increased – the success of the plebiscite. Most members of all social groups willingly voted in favour of the new regime.

There were 7,439,216 votes in favour of the establishment of a presidential regime; 640,737 votes against; and about 1,500,000 abstentions. The main centres of opposition were the large towns, and some Republican areas in the east and the Midi. Workers and artisans were evidently not as likely to vote in favour of Louis-Napoléon as were other social groups.

A year later another plebiscite gave the consent of the people, even more overwhelmingly, to the re-establishment of the empire, but the Republic had disappeared in all but name in December 1851.

The year 1848 in France and the conflicts that ensued were thus terminated by an Imperial dictatorship. Louis-Napoléon in all probability wished to do something to help all social groups and to reduce their mutual hatreds, but his first priority had to be to satisfy those who had supported his action and who provided the key personnel for the state machine. If the aristocracy, and the upper and middle middle-classes had resigned their political power into his hands, they still possessed wealth, eminence and social authority.

The experience of the Second Republic had stimulated the development of political consciousness in all social groups. For the wealthy it served as an awful warning of the social revolution that could smash their world. They had sought, and would repeatedly seek in the future, the protection of authoritarian government and brutal military repression. If under the authoritarian empire the masses relapsed into apathy, the experience and the hopes generated during the Republic would not entirely be forgotten. Universal suffrage survived and, during the empire, even if its use was perverted by government manipulation, it facilitated the political education of the masses. The Third Republic would eventually give due recognition to the France of the lower-middle classes, artisans and peasants, recognizing them, in a world which had begun to change more rapidly, not as a menace but as a source of stability.

Note on the documents

Any period of Revolution is of special interest to the historian. At such times the relaxation of normal constraints, the hopes offered, the anxieties experienced all contribute to people's greater awareness of politics, in the widest sense of the word, and provoke their greater willingness to create, write, act. Paradoxically, periods of intense repression – such as followed the June insurrection, for instance, or the *coup d'état* – also offer more information to the historian than do calmer times. Here, however, the information is often provided by prisoners under interrogation, or by hysterical Conservatives, and must accordingly be treated with great caution.

The documents and extracts that follow (best read in conjunction with the relevant chronological section of the Introduction) were chosen with the aim of presenting an insight into the behaviour and ideas of the major interest-groups active in 1848. They reflect the views of individuals with varying backgrounds and varying degrees of literacy. It is unavoidable that the situations and activity of peasants, workers and of underground political organizations are to a large extent represented not by their own words but by those of the agencies of government. They themselves committed little to paper, and when they did speak it was often in circumstances (e.g., under interrogation) where a desire to conceal the truth was likely. From the mass of available material, then, the historian has to select with great care those documents which he feels best embody the reality of a period, the contemporary consciousness of events that affected people's lives and the world in which they lived.

Part One
February–June 1848

The government success in the election of 1846 had discouraged hope of electoral reform by means of parliamentary action. Indeed, in 1847 two moderate proposals for an extension of the suffrage were rejected by a majority of deputies. The opposition therefore took the initiative, organizing a nationwide campaign to arouse public opinion and organizing a series of banquets (some fifty were held in twenty-eight departments) at which toasts and proposals for reform could be made. In a situation of economic crisis, interest in 'the social problem' made the proposals at a number of these banquets more radical, and participation more democratic, than many of the campaign's organizers would have wished.

The final banquet in Paris was planned in response to the speech from the throne at the end of December 1847 (in which it was made clear that a policy of rejecting reform would continue), and to an unfavourable parliamentary vote on 12 February 1848. Initially, the banquet was to be held in the 12th arrondissement on a Sunday. But with popular interest increasing, the organizers decided instead to hold it on a Monday in a place near the Champs-Elysées, in order to limit popular participation. Probably to the relief of its moderate organizers, the government banned the banquet. But more radical, more anonymous figures called instead for a mass demonstration on 22 February to march from the Place de la Madeleine to the Champs-Elysées. The unlikely result of this development was Revolution.

1 The development of a revolutionary situation

There is a great disquiet in Paris. The funds are falling every day. In politics, people have stopped being reasonable. They are overcome by the consequence of their principles and dragged along in their wake. Now it is events that speak loud. For seventeen years, efforts have been made to stop revolution breaking out in France, and now revolution is feared everywhere.

From *La Gazette de France*, 16 January 1848.

'A DAY OF FATE'
The 12th *arrondissement* of Paris had organized a banquet. The opposition had promised to maintain its political rights by assisting in the celebration. The banquet was to take place on 20 February.

Cartoon by Cham, making fun of the banquet campaign of 1847–48.
Ledru-Rollin beats the big drum.

The ministry declined to adopt force in opposing it, determining rather to establish the offence by a commissary of police, and then to bring it for judgment to the tribunals. The opposition was unanimous in accepting the contest on that ground. All was in preparation for this pacific demonstration.

The evening preceding the day appointed for the banquet, the ministry, alarmed at an invitation given by the impatient Republicans to the unarmed national guards, declared at the tribune that it retracted its concessions and would put down the demonstration by force.

M. Barrot immediately convoked the constitutional opposition at his own house for deliberation. It was there proposed to yield before the violent resolution of the government; M. Barrot and his friends fell in with this proposal.

The government, however, foreseeing the events that might arise from such an agitation and tension of the public mind, had drawn a large number of troops into Paris or around it. They were rated at fifty-five thousand men. The artillery of Vincennes had orders to present itself on the first summons at the faubourg St Antoine. By dispositions carefully studied, and made as far back as 1830, in anticipation of insurrection, posts had been assigned to different bodies in the various quarters of the city. Each body of insurgents, hemmed in, or intercepted by these posts, would be withheld from joining others.

The night [of 21/22 February] was passed in silence – the silence of a city reflecting before action. The morning did not prognosticate a day of fate. There were no arms concealed under the garments; no rage was painted upon men's countenances; curious and inoffensive crowds continually moved along the boulevards, gathering numbers as they went; other crowds streamed from the suburbs of Paris; they appeared, however, rather to observe what was passing than to meditate any act. The event seems to have been engendered by the curiosity that attended it.

The youths of the schools, ever the vanguard in revolutions, assembled in groups from various quarters of the city, and gathering numbers and courage as they rolled along chanting the *Marseillaise*, they directed their course to the Place de la Madeleine. The electrified people responded to the hymn. The column increased, crossed the Place de la Concorde, passed the Pont Royal, forced the palisades of the deserted chamber of deputies, and spread without a leader or a specific object into the gardens of the palace and upon the quays. A regiment of dragoons advanced, and easily, and unresisted, dispersed the youths. The infantry next arrived; the artillery took its position in the Rue de Bourgogne; the bridge was defended by the military.

The deputies, saddened but not disquieted, assembled in their hall without being subjected to insult; they ascended the steps of the portico which faces the bridge, and from thence contemplated the increasing force at the disposal of government, and the advanced waves of the multitude which the cavalry were pushing back in the Rue Royale. No cries were heard, not a single shot. The band of a regiment of chasseurs played its pacific notes before the palisades of the chamber of deputies. . . .

The day, short and gloomy as one of winter, beheld the wandering crowds augment, and some barricades arise, staking out the field of this revolutionary conflict.

Committees of insurrection sat constantly in the secret societies, and in the offices of the Republican journals. We are ignorant of what passed there. They were probably rather engaged in observation than in action. The limited power of a conspirator, who has but scanty numbers at his disposal, only possesses influence as it ministers to a sentiment generally entertained, or a pre-existing passion. . . .

Alphonse de Lamartine, *Histoire de la révolution de 1848*.

⋯ people in the offices of the newspaper La
⋯ *ry 1848,* It was . . . resolved that each
⋯ and with his hands in his pockets,
⋯ the course of events, and to gain
⋯ e of an outbreak, each member
⋯ *La Réforme,* to organize the
⋯ publican character.

L.⋯

THE RISI⋯ ⋯UARY

Night fell, a⋯ ⋯u had been spilt. That night was silent, like the day, but restless, as ⋯ ⋯e eve of a great event. The rumour of a probable change of the ministry, who were relaxing their hold of power, reassured the citizens in some degree. The troops bivouacked in the streets and open spaces. Some wooden chairs and benches belonging to the Champs-Elysées, which had been set on fire by boys, illuminated the horizon, and disclosed the disorder of the scene. The government was everywhere in possession of the streets of Paris, except in a kind of citadel fortified by the nature of the buildings, and of the narrow, tortuous streets, around the cloisters of St Méry, in the centre of Paris.

There some indefatigable and intrepid Republicans, who had eyes for every circumstance and despaired of nothing, had concentrated themselves, either by preconcerted plan, or by the revolutionary instinct that is spontaneous and common in its operation. Their very leaders disapproved their obstinacy and temerity, as they were at most not more than four or five hundred in number. Another detachment of Republicans, altogether without leaders, disarmed the national guards of the Batignolles during the night, burned the station at the barrier,[1] and fortified themselves in a neighbouring quarter, where they awaited the event. No attempt was made to dislodge them.

At break of day, the roads which led to the several gates of Paris were covered with columns of cavalry, infantry, and artillery, summoned by the orders of government. These troops presented an imposing effect; they were obedient and in perfect discipline, but silent and dejected. . . . They successively took up positions in the quarters where the multitude of Paris chiefly reside. The mob did not combat in mass on any point. Scattered groups attacked and disarmed isolated posts, forced their entrance into armourers' shops, and from concealed situations fired random shots at the troops.

[1] The post at which the *octroi,* the internal customs duty, was paid.

Barricades, radiating from a centre by the church of St Méry, were raised at intervals, and built and multiplied almost before the very faces of the soldiers: they were no sooner erected than abandoned. The troops had only stones to oppose. The battle was a silent one – its progress was felt; its sound unheard.

The national guard,[1] summoned by the call to arms, was assembling legion by legion. It preserved a neutrality, or limited its manifestations to an interference between the troops and the people, whilst it loudly demanded the dismissal of the ministry, and reform. Thus the national guard became the shield of the Revolution.

Such, on the dawn of 24 February, was the state of Paris. The troops, wearied by seeing no enemy, though they were the object of universal hostility, remained at their posts, unwavering but dejected. . . . At the exit of the principal streets might be seen groups of cavalry, enveloped in their grey cloaks and with naked sabre in hand. They had been in the same spot, and had maintained the same position, for thirty-six hours; their horses slept under them, and they themselves shivered from cold and hunger. . . .

Few people were in the streets. They seemed to leave their battle to be fought by the invisible spirit of the Revolution, and by that small number of obstinate combatants who were dying for the cause in the heart of Paris. . . .

The fate of the day was at the disposal of the national guard. Hitherto the government had held back from testing the doubtful allegiance of this body by requiring it to take an active part in the event, and fire upon the Parisian people. . . .

The national guard, called to arms on the morning of 24 February, and ordered to interpose between the people and the troops of the line, obeyed the summons slowly and with indecision.

In the prolonged movement of the people the guard saw an anti-ministerial demonstration, an armed petition in favour of electoral reform, which it was far from disapproving, and which it secretly favoured. . . .

Nor was the guard alarmed to see the people vote with firearms against the worn-out system of the king. Louis-Philippe had declined in its affections as he had declined in years. His wisdom appeared to the Parisians petrified into obstinacy; . . .

In the judgment of the national guard, the consequences of the rising would be confined to a change of ministry forced upon the king by the attitude of the people, which would admit the present opposition, in the persons of M. Thiers and M. Odilon Barrot, to the conduct of affairs; to a moderate reform of the electoral law. . . . In fine, the national guard

---

[1] At this time the guards, since they were expected to meet the cost of their equipment, were mainly of the middle classes.

imagined itself introducing the opposition to power, when in fact it was introducing Revolution to France. . . . On the evening of 23 February, shortly after the decline of day, the populace, assured of a change of ministry, rolled along the boulevards and the streets, hailing with applause the illuminations that lighted up the façades of the houses.

A feeling of peaceful joy filled the breasts of the citizens. There was a sort of tacit proclamation of reconciliation between king and people, after an outburst of anger. It was known that the king, shaken but not subdued, had successively summoned to the Tuileries M. Molé, M. Thiers, and M. Barrot.

A small number of combatants concentrated in the quarter of Paris that by its obliquity and the narrowness and crookedness of its streets forms the natural citadel of insurrection, preserved a hostile attitude and impregnable position. These men were almost all veterans of the Republic, formed to voluntary discipline in the secret societies of the two monarchies, inured to conflict, and even martyrdom, in the days when Paris had been inundated with blood, and witnessed a contest for the establishment of the monarchy. None knew by whom they were commanded. Their invisible chief had neither name nor rank. . . . It was that disinterested fanaticism, and that cold courage, which delights to die if, in that death, posterity may find the germ of amelioration and of life. To men like these, two other species of combatants gave their adherence, classes who ever throw themselves into the tumultuous movements of sedition: savage natures, who luxuriate in blood and delight in death; and frivolous natures, who storm attracts and rivets, the genuine children of Paris. But this nucleus did not enlarge. It kept watch in silence, musket in hand. It was satisfied thus to give time for the general rise.

No symptoms of this rise appeared; a war cry was necessary to excite it – a cry of horror to sow fury and vengeance in that floating mass of population who are equally ready to retire to their dwellings, or to sally from them for the subversion of the government. A few silent groups alone assembled here and there at the extremity of the faubourgs of the Temple and of St Antoine. Other groups, composed of few individuals, appeared at the mouth of the streets which lead from the Chaussée d'Antin on to the boulevards.

These two classes exhibited a characteristic difference of air and costume. The one was composed of young men belonging to the rich and refined mercantile classes, to the schools, to trade, to the national guard, to literature, and more particularly to the periodical press. These harangued the people, inflamed popular indignation against the king, the minister, and the chambers; spoke of the humiliation of France before the foreigner, of the diplomatic treasons of the court, and the insolent corruption and servility of deputies, who had sold themselves to the sovereign will of

Louis-Philippe; they openly gave out the names of popular ministers whom insurrection was to thrust upon the Tuileries. The numerous promenaders and bystanders, whose curiosity was excited by whatever was new, crowded around these orators, and applauded their expressions. The other class was composed of the lower orders, summoned within the last two days, from their shops, by the sound of firing; clad in their working dress, with their blue shirts open, and their hands still blackened with the smoke of the forge. These came down in silence, in little knots, skirting the walls of those streets which open upon Clichy, la Villette and the Canal de l'Ourcq. One or two workmen, better dressed than the rest, with long skirted cloth coats, walked before them, addressed them in a low tone, and seemed to be giving them the word of command. These were the heads of the sections of the Rights of Man and of Families.[1]

Alphonse de Lamartine, *Histoire de la révolution de 1848.*

FROM RISING TO RIOT

Nine-tenths of the crowd out there on the streets were the people who love to stand and gawp. There was also a sprinkling of those sinister patriots – bandits who play on a crowd's feelings. The majority of the people on the square were in overalls and they formed groups. The bourgeois came and went. . . .

Though they did not yet constitute any real threat, the dense crowds on the square worried the authorities, who called out the cavalry to disperse the people. The most turbulent crowds were at the bottom of the Champs-Elysées by the river. They were driven back several times into the trees, but they could not be broken up. There was a group of those vicious and shameless children there – the *gamins de Paris* as they are called – who are in the forefront of every riot. When the cavalrymen were returning to their positions after a charge, these little rascals hurled stones at their backs.

. . . Contact with armed troops, excitement transmitted from person to person among those who had arrived there with no hostile intent yet who came to believe they were facing their enemies, a few sabres seen flashing in the air, and provocative murmurs from demagogues dotted about in the crowd – all this eventually excited a certain number of extremists. . . . The example set by the urchins and that excitement generated by a rioting mob soon led to frightful assaults. . . .

Lucien de la Hodde, *Histoire des sociétés secrètes et du parti républicain de 1830 à 1848.*

[1] Republican secret societies.

About six o'clock in the evening, a little column of Republicans, of the younger trading population, issued from the Rue Lepelletier, and formed a silent group before the door of *Le National* newspaper, as though it were the appointed place of rendezvous. In all our revolutions, counsel is kept, the word of command is given, and the impulse is directed to the office of a journal. These are the *comitia* of public opinion, the movable tribunes of the people. A long conference took place between the Republicans within and the Republicans without. Expressions, brief but energetic, were exchanged through the low and barred window of the porter's lodge. The group, inspired with the flame they were about to spread, advanced with cries of 'Reform! Down with the ministers! To the boulevard!'. . . .

Two other bodies, in similar silence, advanced at the same instant, like a detached corps, toward a position previously resolved upon. The one seemed to come from the populous and ever-disturbed region of the Boulevard de la Bastille. The other came from the centre of Paris, having formed its nucleus in the office of the journal *La Réforme*. . . .

In the neighbourhood of the café Tortoni, the rendezvous of idlers, the momentum of these bodies was united. They cleared a way through the inquisitive and idle throng, which undulated in the natural way of multitudes to the great thoroughfares of the boulevards. A crowd of inoffensive people followed mechanically in the wake of this silent column. . . .

In the midst of the smoke of torches a red flag waved over the first rank of this multitude. They advanced, multiplying in their progress. A misgiving curiosity attached to this cloud of men, who seemed to carry in their midst the mystery of the day. In front of the Ministry of Foreign Affairs a battalion of the line, drawn up in battle array, with loaded arms and their commander at their head, obstructed the boulevard. Before this hedge of bayonets the column suddenly halts. The flapping of the flag and the flash of the torches frighten the horse of the commander; recoiling in terror on its haunches, the animal plunged into the battalion, which opened to receive its chief. In the confusion of the moment the report of a musket was heard. Did it come, as was said, from some concealed and disaffected hand, fired on the people by one of their own agitators, to revive by the sight of blood the ardour of a struggle which was subsiding? Did it come from the hand of one of the insurgents directed against the troops? Or rather, which is more probable, did it accidentally arise from the motion of a loaded musket, or from the hand of one of the soldiers who supposed that his commander was wounded when he saw his horse take fright? This no man knows. Whether by crime or accident, this explosion created a revolution.

The soldiers, considering themselves attacked, presented their guns; the whole line instantaneously fired. The discharge, reverberating between the lofty houses and in the enclosed streets of the centre of Paris, throws the whole boulevard into excitement. The column of the people of the faubourgs falls, decimated by the balls. The cries of mortal agony and the groans of the wounded mingle with the affrighted shouts of those who had followed from curiosity, and of flying women and children. They rush into the adjoining houses, into the lower streets, and beneath the archways. By the light of torches, half-extinguished in the blood upon the pavement, heaps of dead bodies are perceived strewing the thoroughfare in all directions. The terrified multitude, supposing themselves pursued, fly with cries of vengeance to the Rue Laffitte, leaving between themselves and the battalions an empty space in silence and darkness.

The multitude supposed that they had been treacherously fired upon in the midst of a demonstration of joy and of harmony, occasioned by a change of ministry. They turned their rage against ministers, who were so perfidious as to avenge their fall by torrents of blood, and against a king obstinate enough to fire on that very people which had crowned him at the sacrifice of their lives in 1830. The soldiers, on their part, were thrown into consternation by this undesigned massacre. No one had given orders to fire; nothing had been heard but the word of command to fix bayonets, to resist the fire expected from this sudden movement of the people. Darkness, confusion, chance, and precipitation had done the deed. . . .

Meanwhile the news of this event spread, with a rapidity equal to that of the firing, through the whole line of the boulevard and through the one-half of Paris. The body which had marched from the faubourg, scattered and thrown in confusion for a moment, soon regained order and began to collect its dead. Large wagons . . . were found at hand . . . in order to exhibit through Paris those lifeless bodies, the mere sight of which was destined to rekindle the fury of the people. They collect the corpses and arrange them on the wagons, with their arms hanging over the side, with their wounds exposed and their blood dripping on the wheels. They carry them by torchlight before the office of *Le National*, as the symbol of approaching vengeance exhibited on the cradle of the republic. . . .

During the brief interval of the king's repose, every hour brought accessions of strength to the insurrection. The rumour of a massacre of the people in the boulevards had spread throughout the night, and produced a universal influence. The tocsin had spread to the very suburbs that feverish spasm which makes man incapable either of sleep or of quiet. The whole population was on foot, armed, and prepared for extreme measures. . . . Every minute narrowed the circle of iron and stone with which the barricades enclosed the palace and approaches of the Tuileries. . . .

Between ten and eleven o'clock in the morning, on the Place du Palais Royal, on the Place de la Concorde, and on the two wings of the Louvre, the troops who had been concentrated there were passively listening to the shouts, and gazing at the attacks of the multitude which thronged around

Barricade in the rue St Martin in February 1848.

the palace of the Tuileries and the principal hotels of the government. The men wore an air of astonishment, languor, and dullness. The soldier who is not acting loses all the impulse and enthusiasm of the charge: so much easier is it to brave death than to await it. The national guard, evidently divided, showed themselves in small numbers, endeavouring by exhortation to pacify the crowd and check the violence of the insurgents; but yielding to the pressure from without, to the infection of example, and to their own normal habits of discontent, they formed a line to let the insurrection pass, and cheered it on by their gestures and their cries of *Vive la réforme*! sometimes swelling its numbers by their defection, sanctioning it with their uniforms, and even arming it with their bayonets. . . .

The Place du Carousel and the court of the Tuileries were occupied by horse, foot, and artillery. Within the palace they seemed to be in a state of unconcern, to be expecting that the news of the change of ministry and the promised concessions would of themselves cause the insurrection to subside. . . .

Meanwhile, what was happening at the palace amid the ever rising deluge of the insurrection? The king had given orders that the troops should cease firing, and only maintain their position. . . .

. . . The number of these troops, which was supposed to be at least fifty thousand men, did not exceed an effective body of thirty-five thousand. Deducting the number of soldiers appointed to guard the forts and barracks, and those who were not in active service, from whatever causes, not more than twenty-five thousand fighting men of all arms were found available; – a sufficient corps against scattered and confused masses, not consolidated by any discipline, and which melt away as fast as they form;

but troops already worn out by forty-eight hours of standing in the mud, benumbed with cold, and exhausted with hunger, harassed by doubt, uncertain where lay the right, ashamed of deserting the king, horrified at making war upon the people, and looking for their guidance to the attitude of the national guard, which itself vacillated between the two armies.

Alphonse de Lamartine, *Histoire de la révolution de 1848.*

THE KING GIVES WAY

We found the king wearing his uniform. He was cool and calm – embarrassed rather than intimidated. Taken unawares by a situation he had long ago ceased to expect, he had passed in a few hours from complete confidence in his system, success and power to an appreciation of the need to change, draw back and give way.

It is our attitude, the powerlessness of our will, that humiliates me when I think it over. I account for it by the novel and rapid turn of events. Usually in political matters, however pressing they may be, one always has time to think, weigh up the situation and come to a decision. . . . No chance for anything like that in moments of revolutionary crisis. Events rush along and catch up with you. Everything moves on with dramatic speed. Brusque changes of fortune follow one another all the time. Every minute you discover something unexpected. The time you spend learning about them, understanding them, being surprised or shocked by them, is irretrievably lost for action. You are absorbed like a spectator in the theatre; your curiosity is continually exerted and roused again and again. You cannot think fast enough for reflection. You have no time to tell yourself you must act, ask yourself what to do next or settle on a course of action.

Charles de Rémusat, *Mémoires de ma vie.*

2 *The Revolution successful*

The Republicans whose organization centred on the two newspapers, Le National *and* La Réforme *were able to step into the political vacuum caused by the abdication and flight of Louis-Philippe, and by the unwillingness of the members of the chamber of deputies elected in 1846 to accept governmental responsibility. There was little initial opposition from Conservatives, who hoped that a provisional government including known moderates such as Lamartine would prevent a radicalizing of the Revolution. This very absence of opposition enabled the government to pursue policies aimed at conciliating all social groups. A repetition of the Terror was not necessary. This government was a heterogeneous grouping brought together unexpectedly, almost by the force of circumstances. Its actions reflected its divisions, its lack of formulated policies, its desire to calm the fears of Conservatives, and its wish, stimulated by pressure from crowds in the streets, to do something to better the lives of the poor.*

A THREAT OF PERMANENT REVOLUTION
Citizens!

For three days the people has been shamefully sacrificed by the authorities. As in 1830, it is victorious. But this time it will not lay down its arms. The authorities would only cheat it once more. Only the people is sovereign. It alone can provide itself with a fitting government.

Text of placard found on a barricade at the Collège de France. (Documented in *Les Murailles révolutionnaires de 1848*.)

MODERATION EVEN IN REVOLUTION
To the Workers!

Brothers!

We learn that amid the joy over our triumph, some of our supporters, misled by perfidious suggestions, desire to tarnish the glory of our revolution by excesses which we most energetically condemn. They wish to break the mechanical presses.

Brothers! These people are wrong. Like them we suffer from the turmoil that follows the mechanization of industry. But instead of blaming inventions that reduce toil and increase productivity, we should accuse only selfish, short-sighted governments for our misfortunes.

Things cannot be allowed to continue like this in the future.

Poster dated 25 February 1848. The majority of its twenty-nine signatories were printing workers and associates of the workers' newspaper *L'Atelier*. (Documented in *Les Murailles révolutionnaires de 1848*.)

THE INITIAL IDEALISM OF MODERATE REPUBLICANISM
Never was a victory more rapid, more unexpected.

And after the victory, nothing was more impressive than the good order.

From *Le National*, 25 February 1848. (A majority of the provisional government was closely associated with this newspaper, which adequately represents its views.)

The French Republic has an obligation to organize society on totally new bases. If at present it is the safety anchor for all of us, it, in its turn, is anchored to this ideal of social renewal. Without it nothing firm will ever be established. Nobody can raise any objection to so just a duty. The classes that have for so long been deprived of their birthright are entitled to work, education and a life that includes all the advantages of civilization.

Ibid., 26 February 1848.

CONCILIATION, ORDER AND PATIENCE

The provisional government has great duties in today's circumstances.

On the one hand, it must arouse interest in the maintenance of good order among that considerable number of citizens who, since so far they have been deprived of social rights, perhaps do not yet suspect by what means their legitimate desires will be satisfied. The structure of the Republican government with its simple, regular organs will make every reform and every improvement easy and speedy. These reforms might be jeopardized by haste and impatience. Quiet confidence ought to make it possible to bring them to fruition in the shortest possible time.

On the other hand, the provisional government should take steps to keep the good will that it has already won from those citizens who under the former regime did not desire so radical a change, but who loyally resign themselves to the altered situation. Such people represent a considerable force, and the provisional government should openly offer them reassurances.

Ibid., 27 February 1848.

CONSERVATIVE RESIGNATION

People who did not see Paris that evening, a Paris where all was good order, concord and majesty in the very midst of the sublime disorder of the barricades, will never have any notion of how fine the idea of the sovereignty of the people really is.

From *La Gazette de France*, 27 February 1848.

. . . [On 25 February] I spent the whole afternoon wandering about Paris and was particularly struck by two points: first, I will not say the mainly, but rather the uniquely and exclusively popular character of the recent revolution, and the omnipotence it had given the so-called people – that is to say, the classes who work with their hands – over all other classes.

Paris: reconciliation between Church and Republic. The Tree of Liberty at the Marché des Innocents being blessed by the curé of St Eustache on 26 March 1848.

Secondly, how little hatred, or indeed any other acute feeling, was shown in this first moment of victory by the humble people who had suddenly become the sole masters of power. . . .

Throughout this day in Paris I never saw one of the former agents of authority: not a soldier, nor a gendarme, nor a policeman; even the national guard had vanished. The people alone bore arms, guarded public buildings, watched, commanded and punished; it was an extraordinary and terrible thing to see the whole of this huge city, full of so many riches . . . in the hands of those who owned nothing. . . .

In these days [immediately following the Revolution] I perceived a universal inclination to fit in with the improvisations of fortune and to tame the new master. Great landlords delighted to recall that they had always been hostile to the middle class and well disposed to the humble; priests again found the dogma of equality in the gospel and assured us that they had always seen it there; even the middle classes discovered a certain pride in recalling that their fathers had been workers. . . .

Alexis de Tocqueville, *Recollections*.

My first concern was to call in my children. I tried to prepare them for the new situation. Up to now thay have been able to consider themselves among the privileged. Their future was, so to speak, assured; everything was likely to be quite easy for them. Well, things were changing. They were probably going to have to live under indifferent or hostile governments.

Charles de Rémusat, *Mémoires.*

REACTIONS IN THE PROVINCES
Universal astonishment was caused here by this sudden and unexpected news of Revolution.

From a report of the Procureur-général at Aix,
28 February 1848 (Archives national, BB[30] 358).

The new order of things is accepted everywhere. Everywhere it is understood that, if confusion and anarchy are to be avoided, support must be given to the provisional government. . . . But these rather backward people in the south do not feel any affection for it.

Ibid., 2 March 1848.

THE ARMY
I decided to give my support to the Republic when I learned that a proportion of the men who had seized power were struggling in the Hôtel-de-Ville against anarchistic passions, when I saw that the government that had been born at the barricades was proclaiming the great principles of social order. My confidence was great in the early days. Lamartine's high views were and still are a guarantee. Many other members of the government are behind him.

Marechal Bugeaud, duc d'Isly, in a letter to General
Pelissier, 3 April 1848.

THE CHURCH
Dearly beloved Colleagues,

You will all be aware of the political changes that have occurred in France. We who are always concerned with eternal matters will not be surprised to hear it said that, in its justice, the hand of God overturns thrones and brings crowned heads to nought.

Above, *February 1848:
a crowd of insurgents led
by a student of the École
Polytechnique rescues a
crucifix from desecration
during the sacking of the
Tuileries and transports
it to the church of
Saint-Roch.*

Left, *against demands for
its replacement by the
red flag, Lamartine
successfully pleads for the
retention of the tricolour,
symbol of the glories of
the First Republic and
Empire.*

Give a lead to the faithful in obedience and submission to the Republic. You often used to long for that liberty which makes our brothers in the United States of America so happy. This liberty will now be yours.

Concern yourself always with the poor; play your part in any measures that can improve the lot of the workers.

Cardinal de Bonald, archbishop of Lyon, in a circular
letter to the clergy of his diocese, 27 February 1848.
(Documented in *Les Murailles révolutionnaires de 1848.*)

3 Measures of the provisional government

One of the measures of the provisional government, the establishment of the national workshops, was to be a cause of conflict in the near future. Their very existence represented the ambiguity of the provisional government's position. The decree recognized a right to work, and so seemed to accord recognition to the ideas of Louis Blanc, a member of the government. It seemed to promise something permanent, namely an end to the insecurity of the worker's life. Yet in the way it was organized, in the way work was actually provided, and, no doubt, in the intentions of some other members of the government, it followed in the traditions of charity workshops that gave temporary relief to the unemployed during a crisis, partly for humanitarian reasons, partly because otherwise they might cause disorder in the streets. Thus what was established was an expedient, and an expensive one at that, designed to facilitate social control.

THE RIGHT TO WORK

The provisional government of the French Republic undertakes to guarantee the workers' livelihood through work.

It undertakes to guarantee work for every citizen.

It recognizes that workers should form associations so that they may enjoy the proper profits arising from their toil.

Government decision of 25 February 1848; published in
Le Moniteur, 26 February 1848.

AMBIGUOUS CHARACTER OF THE NATIONAL WORKSHOPS

When as a result of abnormal conditions large numbers of workers lose their normal jobs, the opening of temporary national workshops appears a natural expedient both as a means of helping those in misfortune and of maintaining order in society. It is a measure which has always been turned to in times of public disturbance.

From *Le Constitutionnel*, 29 February 1848.

Whereas the Revolution brought about by the people should be to the people's benefit;

Whereas the time has come to put an end to the workers' long and iniquitous sufferings;

Whereas the question of work is of supreme importance;

Whereas there is no problem that is greater or more worthy of a Republican government's concern;

Whereas it is pre-eminently for France to study keenly to resolve a problem manifested in this day and age in all the industrial nations of Europe;

Whereas means must be found without the least delay to guarantee to the people the proper fruits of their toil;

The provisional government of the Republic decrees that:

A standing committee, to be called the Government Committee for the Workers, shall be appointed with the express and specific task of concerning itself with the workers' problems.

To demonstrate what importance the provisional government of the Republic attaches to the solution of this major problem, it nominates as Chairman of the Government Committee for the Workers one of its own members, M. Louis Blanc, and, as vice-chairman, another of its members, M. Albert, who is himself a worker.

Workers will be invited to join the committee.

The committee will sit in the Luxembourg palace.

Government decision of 28 February 1848; published in
Le Moniteur, 29 February 1848.

REDUCTION OF WORKING HOURS

On the report of the Government Committee for the Workers, the provisional government decrees:

1. That excessively long manual work does not merely ruin the workers' health; since it also prevents him from developing his mind it is an insult to human dignity. The working day is therefore shortened by one hour.

Accordingly, in Paris, where the working day used to be eleven hours, it is reduced to ten, and in the provinces, where it has hitherto been twelve hours, it is reduced to eleven.

2. The employment of workers by working-class sub-contractors, called *marchandeurs* or *tâcherons*[1] is essentially unjust, vexatious and contrary to

[1] The *marchandeurs* or *tâcherons* contracted to supply labour. They made a profit on the difference between the money they received from the contractor and the wages they paid to workers. It was in their interest to persuade workers to compete between themselves for work, and thus to force down wages.

the ideals of fraternity. Accordingly the right of sub-contractors of this sort to organize labour is abolished.

Government decision of 2 March 1848; published in
Le Moniteur, 3 March 1848.

THE POLITICAL FRAMEWORK

Decreed:

That the representatives of the people shall number nine hundred.

That suffrage shall be direct, universal, without any property qualification.

That all Frenchmen aged twenty-one years or more shall be electors, and all Frenchmen aged twenty-five years or more shall be eligible.

That the poll shall be secret.

Government decision of 4 March; published in
Le Moniteur, 5 March 1848.

FOREIGN POLICY: THE REPUBLIC MEANS PEACE

The proclamation of the French Republic is not an act of aggression against any sort of government in the world. There are differences between forms of government which are as legitimate as the different sorts of character, of geographical situation, and of intellectual, moral and material development seen in various nations.

War is therefore not a principle of the French Republic.

Alphonse de Lamartine, minister for foreign affairs, in a
circular letter to French diplomatic agents. (Documented
in *Les Murailles révolutionnaires de 1848*.)

ABOLITION OF SLAVERY[1]

The provisional government decrees:

Article 1. Slavery is totally abolished throughout the French colonies and possessions.

Government decision of 27 April 1848; published in
Le Moniteur, 2 May 1848.

[1] Slavery in the French colonies was abolished by decree of the Convention on 16 Pluviose year II (4 February 1794), but re-established by Bonaparte in 1802. The slave trade was banned on 29 March 1815, and slaves finally emancipated in 1848.

The liberation of the slaves at Réunion, 20 December 1848.

THE WEAKNESS OF THE PROVISIONAL GOVERNMENT

It was a farrago of Conservatives, doctrinaires, Jacobins, Socialists, all talking their own private language. Since they had such difficulty in settling the smallest matter of policy it would have been miraculous if they had finally agreed over something like a revolution.

P.-J. Proudhon, *Les Confessions d'un révolutionnaire.*

THE LOST OPPORTUNITY

The Republic had . . . no opposition to overcome either from within or from without. Never has any government been in so strong a position as the February government. It could set up the Republic on broad, firm foundations without any danger of resistance. Energetic measures and radical reforms were expected: the People wanted them, the privileged classes were resigned to them. But the men in power behaved as if astonished by their new eminence. . . . Instead of relying on the People's support, they seemed to have but one preoccupation – the desire to make themselves acceptable to the bourgeoisie.

Louis Ménard, *Prologue d'une Révolution.*

4 The promise of a new era for the workers

PEACEFUL REFORM OR...

If some citizens, suffering because of the competition from powerful interests, were to let themselves be dragged into machine-breaking they would be mistaking their real enemies. Their enemy is not the economical and highly productive machine. It is the feudal–industrial government that, in order to found its power on the slavery of hunger, has cheapened labour and refused the workers both credit and the right of association.

With the institutions that should flow from government based on the sovereignty of the people and subject to control by the people, these vices will be a thing of the past. Machines are above all a potent force for revolution and democracy. Instead of crushing democracy and revolution, as in the era of feudal industry, they should set the people free.

From *La Réforme*, 26 February 1848.

...FURTHER REVOLUTION? REPUBLICANS DIVIDED

France is not Republican. The Revolution that has just passed is nothing more than a happy surprise. If today we endeavour to bring into power men who have been compromised in the eyes of the bourgeoisie because they have been found guilty of political offences, the provinces will become frightened. They will remember the Terror – and the Convention – and may bring back the king from flight. The national guard itself has only been an unwilling accomplice; it is composed of timid shopkeepers who tomorrow may well put an end to all that they allowed to happen amid those cries of 'Long live the Republic!' Leave the men in the Hôtel-de-Ville to their impotence; their feebleness is a sure sign of their fall. Their power is but ephemeral: we – we have the people and the clubs,[1] where we shall organize them in revolutionary fashion, as was the way of the Jacobins of old.

Let us have enough sense to wait a few days more – then the revolution will be ours!

Auguste Blanqui, speech of 25 February 1848 given at the Club du Prado (*see* Alphonse Lucas, *Les Clubs et les clubistes*).

[1] Within a month of the Revolution, about 250 clubs for political discussion had been created in Paris, and many in the provinces. The ideas expressed in them were often extreme, but as bases for political organization they proved ineffective.

5 *The Conservative conception of the Republic*

The re-establishment of order is now the prime preoccupation of all decent folk. To whatever party they belong, whatever opinion they espouse, people everywhere feel the need for peace and quiet again. This feeling is all the stronger in Paris since quite large numbers of malefactors, so as to profit from the commotion that has just occurred and the vacuum that is always left behind by the collapse of a government, have formed armed bands to masquerade as national guard patrols. This has resulted in many acts of violence and many instances of theft and looting, to the detriment of both people and property.

From *Le Constitutionnel*, 29 February 1848.

6 *The call for continuous public action*

Republicans!

Winning is not everything. The people has not yet gathered the fruits of its victory, but if this is to be done swiftly and surely, a closer and more energetic watch must be kept.

Do not lose sight of the fact, citizens, that the enemies of the Revolution are striving to increase the difficulties surrounding the government and thus prevent it from accomplishing with due rapidity the great duties imposed upon it in the present circumstances. . . .

We must come together, unite. Accordingly we call on the citizens immediately to form in every *arrondissement* popular assemblies that will co-operate in facilitating and strengthening the government's actions while showing in what direction it should go by acting continuously as organs for the expression of public opinion.

Poster issued by the Société populaire of the 11th
arrondissement, dated 1 March 1848. (Documented in
Les Murailles révolutionnaires de 1848.)

THE STATUTES OF A POPULAR ORGANIZATION
Society for the Rights of Man and of the Citizen.
The aims of the society are:

1. To defend the people's rights, the exercise of which was confirmed by the February Revolution.

2. To ensure that all the social consequences of the Revolution are followed up.

'The Declaration of the Rights of Man', formulated by Robespierre in 1793, is the basis of its thoughts.

Consequently, in the social revolution that is starting the Society for the Rights of Man takes its stance henceforth between the *pariahs* and *privileged* classes of the old society. To the former it will say: Remain united, but calm: that is where your strength lies. Your numbers are such that a mere demonstration of your will will suffice to obtain what you desire. It is also such that you cannot desire anything but what is right. Your voice and will are the voice and will of God.

To the others, the Society says: The old social system has disappeared. The reign of privilege and exploitation has gone. If under the former social system you won certain privileges in a legal manner, do not take advantage of them. For those laws were your handiwork. The vast majority of your brothers had no part in their formulation: therefore they are not obliged to respect them. Join the cause, then, for you must seek pardon of those whose interests you sacrificed for too long. If now, despite this promise of pardon, you persist in isolating yourself in order to defend the former social order, you will discover our well organized sections there in the vanguard when the struggle begins. And your brothers will not talk of *pardon* then, but only of JUSTICE!

Documented in *Les Murailles révolutionnaires de 1848*.

7 *Radical Republican proposals for action*

STATE INTERVENTION IN THE ECONOMY

At the present moment the holders of capital are refusing to serve their function as the source of economic life and work. Or perhaps they cannot. It makes no difference. They are adopting, perhaps without due consideration, a dangerous and fatal course. The state must supplant them in this function which they are abandoning. The state must become banker and discount at low interest rates.

The state must open workshops for the men left idle because industry has failed.

From *La Réforme*, 8 March 1848.

THE NEED TO PURGE THE BUREAUCRACY

We shall have to ask again why almost all the hierarchical columns of the monarchy have been left standing with all those administrators who grew old in the service of the monarchy. The officials in the ministries will, indeed, if they keep their superior positions, keep their sovereign influence and the Revolution may . . . be strangled.

From 'La Réforme, 8 March 1848.

3 Workers' demands

UNREALISTIC EXPECTATIONS
Those among the workers who had never given a hang for their liberty or their rights suddenly became astonishingly demanding. No measure by the provisional government could satisfy them.

Martin Nadaud, *Mémoires de Léonard*.

AN EXAGGERATED SENSE OF THEIR OWN STRENGTH
Louis-Philippe's government was so identified in everybody's mind with the middle class that the workers imagined they had beaten the bourgeoisie on 24 February. This victory, won so easily because of the lack of resistance and because of positive help from the national guard, had given them an exaggerated notion of their powers. Because of all the official statements by the provisional government, the speeches and proclamations, and the prudent reserve of the other citizens, this notion later gave way to sheer, wild delight.

Odilon Barrot, *Mémoires posthumes*, vol. II.

THE INFLUENCE OF THE CLUBS
The clubs exercised a lively fascination over the public in Paris, which likes novelty and public speaking and is not averse to scandal. But their influence was neither uniform nor salutary. The voice of serious men could rarely dominate the racket put up by the madmen. Sound political advice made little headway against the flattery and perfidious exaggerations with which the people's ears were beginning to be poisoned. Instead of teaching the proletariat the great new truths about democratic institutions and the profound significance of the sovereignty of the people, speakers in most of the clubs inspired the pernicious idea of imitating the Jacobins. The proletariat was taught the language of another age which they had forgotten. Notions of revolutionary despotism were wakened.

Daniel Stern, *Histoire de la révolution de 1848*, vol. II.

CLUBS AND POLITICAL DEBATE IN THE PROVINCES
The clubs stirred up the department more and more. Each town had several, some supported by crypto-royalists, others by democrats of varying hues. The setting up of these clubs was certainly excellent, but the effect was disappointing. They should have been used as an instrument of propa-

ganda, in order to teach the people the truth, to discuss plans for reform for immediate implementation, and to create intelligent and convinced defenders of the Republic. Nothing of the kind was done. The platform was normally occupied only by speechifyers without ideas whose object was to work up the audience with grand phrases and gestures and win applause. In this it was almost certain that the honours of the meeting would go to the orators whose delivery was the most violent and whose speeches were almost always the emptiest. The clubs, I regret to say, usually served only to give prominence to disappointing mediocrities while they could and should have been a real means of educating the people.

Pierre Joigneaux, *Souvenirs historiques.*

9 Revolutionary Republicanism

Without social reform, there can be no real Republic.

If the national assembly lacked the courage to abolish the proletariat[1] then we should have to continue, in the name of equality, the Revolution we started in the name of liberty.

From *La Vraie République*, 26 March 1848.

Where is the madman – or the charlatan – who claims that the liberty of the proletariat can be assured without the reorganization of property? What produces civil and political liberty, what makes it a real living thing instead of a chimerical and perfidious abstraction, is property. It follows that all men must be made property-owners or that property must be socialized in such a manner that no citizen depends materially on any other. There is no other road to salvation. . . .

From *Le Peuple Souverain*, 26 March 1848.

Proudhon, caricature, 1848.

[1] Not in the Marxist sense, but through a wider distribution of property, in land and capital, by organizing cheap credit and, in the case of urban workers, by facilitating the establishment of producer–co-operatives.

10 *Petition for the postponement of the election of a constituent assembly*

Blanqui twice petitioned for postponement of the election of a constituent assembly, stressing the need for time to educate the masses and remove them from the influence of employers, Notables and clergy The provisional government conceded a limited postponement. This satisfied no one, and indeed contributed to its being discredited in the eyes of both moderates and conservatives. The possibilities of Republican electoral successes were reduced, since the established Notables gained time to recover from the shock of Revolution, and to organize themselves.

Citizens, we demand the adjournment of the elections for the constituent assembly and the national guard. These elections would be derisory.

In the towns, the working classes, conditioned to subjugation by long years of repression and poverty, would take no part in the voting or else they would be led to the polls by their masters like blind cattle.

Out in the countryside, all the influence is in the hands of the clergy and of the aristocrats.

The people do not know; yet know they must. This is not a task to be accomplished in a day or even a month. When counter-revolution alone has had the right to speak for half a century, is it too much to give perhaps a year to liberty?

Enlightenment must reach even the tiniest hamlets. The workers must lift up their heads which have been bowed by servitude and recover from that state of prostration and stupor in which they used to be kept by powerful oppressive interests.

From *Deuxième pétition pour l'ajournement des élections*,
by the Société républicaine centrale, issued on 14 March
1848. (Blanqui was a leading figure in this club.)

11 *Conservative fears*

DISORDER IN THE TOWNS

The question of the day is purely a social one. It cannot be discussed freely when you are faced with the mob. It is no longer a matter of theory but of brute force, which is testing its strength in the streets of Paris and which brooks no opposition.

The population of our kings in overalls grows larger day by day. They strut about the streets, sometimes alone, sometimes in great masses, to take part in all manner of demonstrations which are, of course, always directed against law and order. . . . Everything must be razed to the ground, nothing must remain upright. That's what they want, these thousand upon thousand of tyrants who reign over us.

R. Apponyi, *Journal*, entry under 17 March 1848.

UNREST IN THE COUNTRYSIDE
Our rural communes, though they seemed peaceful, were not, however, totally cut off from the general commotion. Without being ready for it, without understanding at all, the peasants realized that what had just happened was of great importance to the poor, that they were going to have an important part to play and that their lives would be changed. I found these ideas were held even at Lafitte, where everybody was, however, voting for me. They came and sang the *Marseillaise* in my garden, and, if my relationship with our workpeople remained good, it was no longer the same thing. Their tone – and mine – had altered.

Charles de Rémusat, *Mémoires*.

LACK OF CONFIDENCE IN THE PROVISIONAL GOVERNMENT
All these revolutionary demonstrations, these parades in the streets, and these illuminations, which we are forced to permit, destroy the little confidence that remains in the government, whose very members fail to get on with one another!

Daumier laughs at the fear of a bourgeois couple frightened by children at play, though fear of armed insurrection was a very real aspect of the social situation.

The speeches in the clubs are alarming, terrible. There is talk only of confiscation and massacres. Everything is leading up to another Terror.

R. Apponyi, *Journal*, entry under 19 March 1848.

THE ARMY'S INABILITY TO GUARANTEE ORDER
Some regiments are handing in their arms. Others are sending their officers packing. There are even soldiers who refuse to do duty in the guard-room. What a pretty pickle! And what a condition for an army to be in!

Maréchal de Castellane, *Journal*, entry under 16 March 1848.

2 *The creation of a Conservative alliance*

[in the department of Manche] . . . the Revolution was hardly noticed at first. . . . The upper classes immediately bent beneath the blow, and the lower classes scarcely felt it. . . . But when they began to hear talk of the disorder prevailing in Paris, new taxes to be imposed, and the fear of a general war; when, too, they saw trade coming to a standstill and money apparently vanishing underground; and especially when they heard that the principle of property was being attacked, they realized that something more than Louis-Philippe was at stake.

The fear, which in the beginning had been confined to the upper level of society, now descended to the lowest of the working class, and a universal terror gripped the countryside. . . . For although some sort of demagogic agitation prevailed among the workers in the towns, in the country all the landowners, whatever their origin, antecedents, education or means, had come together and seemed to form a single unit: all the old political hatreds and rivalries of caste and wealth had vanished. Neither jealousy nor pride separated the peasant from the rich man any longer, nor the bourgeois from the gentleman; instead, there was mutual confidence, respect and goodwill. Ownership constitutes a sort of fraternity linking all who had anything: the richest were the elder brothers and the less prosperous the younger; but all thought themselves brothers, having a common inheritance to defend. . . . Experience has proved that the union was not as close as it seemed to be, has shown that the old parties and the various classes were juxtaposed rather than mingled; fear had acted upon them as physical pressure might on very hard substances, forcing them to hold together while the compression continued, but leaving them to fall apart when it was relaxed.

Alexis de Tocqueville, *Recollections*.

13 The moderate Republican desire for order

Despite all the patience and gentleness of the authorities toward the workers, I think that stern measures will be needed, and perhaps fighting, too, eventually. The workers abuse their position to bring in completely arbitary laws, and everybody is getting tired of backing down all the time on everything.

Joseph Bergier, *Journal d'un bourgeois de Lyon en 1848*,
entry under 24 March 1848.

14 The provisional government frightens Conservatives

What are your powers? They know no limits.

Agent of a revolutionary authority, you are a revolutionary too. After the people's victory you have a mandate to proclaim and consolidate its work. To accomplish this task, you are invested with its sovereignty; you stand only before your own conscience. You must do what circumstances require for the public good. . . . Republican sentiments must be actively roused. For that, all political duties must be in the hands of reliable, well-meaning men. Prefects and sub-prefects must be changed everywhere. . . .

Your main task is the elections. They ought to save the country. Our future depends on the composition of the assembly. It must be inspired with the Revolutionary spirit. Your watchword everywhere must be: New men – and, so far as possible, they should come forward from the people.

The country is incompletely educated. So it is for you to guide the country.

A. Ledru-Rollin, minister of the interior, in a letter to the
commissaires (who were replacing the prefects) of the
provisional government, dated 12 March 1848.
The letter chiefly succeeded in frightening Conservatives.

15 The forty-five-centime tax

Whereas the well-being of the Republic requires that great aid be given at once to work, industry and commerce;

Whereas it is no less necessary or urgent to reorganize the armed forces of the Republic;

The provisional government decrees that:

There shall be payable immediately, and for the year 1848 only, a tax of *forty-five centimes* on the total amounts for the four direct taxes receivable this year.[1]

The *centimes* on land tax shall be charged only to the owners; notwithstanding any stipulation to the contrary in leases and agreements.

Government decision of 16 March 1848; published in
Le Moniteur, 17 March 1848.

6 Popular disorder in the provinces

This section illustrates the complexity of political situations involving economic protest, traditional folkloric forms of protest and local animosities as responses to national political events. To very many people Revolution, and the liberty it promised, meant an opportunity to express their grievances. Lacking an ideologically based political consciousness, and without political organization, their protest expressed itself in traditional, often violent forms. The relaxation of controls by an unsure administration removed a major obstacle to protest, just as their reimposition, where necessary enforced by use of the army, soon limited the opportunities for protest.

The forest laws[2] – and above all their application in mountainous regions – failed to take into account the first needs of the population. In the middle of forests the people were deprived of wood for heating and building. Because of . . . transport difficulties and the poverty of the majority of these highlanders, wood cannot be purchased elsewhere and brought in. To protect themselves from the rigors of the winter, the elderly and the children were obliged to stay in bed for days on end. To cook the food some inhabitants burned planks, torn up from their houses, and their old furniture.

Hearing the news of events in Paris and of the Revolution that was taking place, the highlanders thought that the forestry regulations were abolished. With shouts of 'Liberty, long live the Republic!' they invaded the forests and threw out the guards. . . .

When the political and social revolution changed the institutions, thus creating new rights and new duties, this seemed to some to mean the right-

---

[1] The four direct taxes were: the land tax; a personal tax based on the estimated rental value of buildings owned; a tax on doors and windows; and the *patente*, a tax paid by industrialists and members of the liberal professions, which was supposed to reflect the scale of their business activity. In fact, much of the tax burden was shouldered by the less well-off by means of indirect taxation.

[2] Designed to prevent over-use and depredation.

ing of every wrong. But for others it was a pretext for paying off old scores and wriggling out of legitimate obligations.

In Mijanès, one of the principal villages in the canton of Querigut (Ariège), two people who possessed a certain fortune became the object of public recriminations and violence. At the death of her father, a retired doctor, Mlle Authier had inherited many unpaid debts. On these she drew only a legitimate interest, but people claimed that most of the debts had mounted up because of usury. The debtors rioted. Those from neighbouring districts joined those in Mijanès. A mob of several hundred armed individuals, marching to the sound of a drum, made its way to Mlle Authier's house, shouting for the return of all the receipts. The doors were broken down, the rooms invaded, the furniture ransacked and smashed. Mlle Authier had escaped, carrying off her most valuable possessions, including her papers.

The next day, the rioters surrounded the house in which Mlle Authier had taken refuge, threatening their creditor with death if she did not hand over their contracts. She had to give way to their violence, and the various documents were handed over. Those debts figuring as a mere reference in the account books were struck out. Thus, in two days, some twenty-five thousand to thirty thousand francs were lost. . . .

From a report of the Procureur-général at Toulouse,
15 April 1848 (Archives nationales, BB[18] 1461).

From time immemorial, the villages in the Bas Rhin department near the forests have enjoyed rights of way and grazing rights in these forests. . . .

Since the promulgation of the forestry code, this state of affairs has totally changed. Not only have the inhabitants whose privileges were not recorded in writing been largely dispossessed, but means have been found, by creating a myriad of difficulties, to prevent them from exercising even the best established rights.

The result has been frightful hardship in those villages whose inhabitants are reduced in large part to cultivating this ungrateful soil which produces little corn and is hardly capable of providing the potatoes necessary for their sustenance.

Through the loss of grazing and of rights of way in the forests the inhabitants have been obliged to give up stock-rearing almost entirely. Villages which twenty-five years ago had a hundred and fifty to two hundred cows and three to four hundred pigs, now have only sixty to eighty cows and five or six pigs.

Taking into consideration the enormous loss resulting from the reduction in numbers of cattle, the outbreak of potato blight which has spoiled, and in some cases even destroyed, these highlanders' staple and sometimes only, crop, it really is surprising that they have been able to survive. Thus they are reduced to the severest privations. Most of the families do not have meat to eat twice a year. In the last two bad years they have been forced to feed on the wild plants they had gathered in the forests.

So it is not surprising that, last year, during the Revolution, these populations, goaded by poverty and seeking to improve their wretched lot, committed certain excesses in the forest.

I would add this: at the time of the elections for president of the Republic, these poor populations all voted as one for Napoléon because they hoped he would restore the forest rights and usages they enjoyed under the emperor. Disappointed hopes on this score, together with the promises made by opposition candidates to restore their forestry rights, were the main cause of the set-back suffered by the supporters of the president at the last elections.

G. Goldenberg, deputy of the Bas-Rhin, in a letter to the minister of justice, dated 12 July 1849[1].

Large groups of labourers were turning up at houses of the landowners or tenants. They came to claim wages of fr. 2·50 a day, which is fr. 0·50 above the rate they used to get.

The origins of the troubles in Lunel (Hérault) lie in the false notions harboured by the working population, especially among the uneducated labourers, as a result of promises made by the February Revolution with regard to the organization of work. Into the assurances given by the government that everybody would be able to earn a living by working the labourers have chosen to read the right to impose their will on the landowners. The labourers have formed groups and claim the right to go and till the soil wherever they wish without the consent and even despite the prohibitions of the landowner or his tenant.

From a report of the Procureur-général at Montpellier, 15 May 1848 (Archives nationales, BB[30] 362).

On the evening of 6 June disturbances occurred in Semur (Côte-d'Or). A mob of vine-growers marched on the residence of the collector of indirect taxes, shouting threats and talking of burning his papers and turning him out of the town. . . . People were exasperated because of the new rate of tax on wine.

Report on the five-day period 11–15 June 1848 by the general officer commanding the 5th military division (Archives historiques du Ministère de la Guerre F[1] 16).

[1] This, part of a plea for the pardon of individuals involved in disturbances of 1848, obviously refers back to the situation that then prevailed.

On 22 May at Rosières (Somme) some eight to nine hundred persons from this commune and others nearby ran through the village with a loaf of bread on a pickaxe, shouting: 'This is what the poor need!' They forced their way into several houses and obliged people to give them alms.

Report on the five-day period 25–31 May 1848 by the
general officer commanding the 3rd military division
(ibid.).

On 11 June a brawl between Catholics and Protestants at Nîmes necessitated the intervention of the army. On 13 and 14 June there were disturbances. Shots were fired: a man was killed. Alarm spread through the city, the troops stood to, and the municipal authorities called out the national guard. The mob dispersed little by little.

Report on the five-day period 10–15 June 1848 by the
general officer commanding the 8th military division
(ibid.).

On 18 May French navvies working on the Dunkirk railway line attacked Belgian workers who, after collecting their pay, returned home. There were about fifty of them.

Report on the five-day period 15–20 May 1848 by the
general officer commanding the 5th military division
(ibid.).

17 *Popular demonstration in Paris: 17 March 1848*

[The demonstrators demanded] the adjournment of elections, an attitude of suspicion toward the future national assembly, acceptance of the principle that troops should be permanently withdrawn from Paris, implicit obedience to the dictatorial will of the masses as expressed by the clubs: in a word, the enslavement of the government, the outlawing of everything in the nation except Paris, and an ill-defined dictatorship to be exercised by the government on condition that this government accept and itself ratify the dictatorship of demagogy which reigned supreme.

Alphonse de Lamartine, *Histoire de la révolution de 1848.*

PROVISIONAL GOVERNMENT'S RESPONSE
TO DEMONSTRATIONS
Citizens, liberty and free discussion are the lifeblood of the Republic. For the Republic clubs are a necessity; for the people they are a right.

So the provisional government has been glad to see the people meeting together in various parts of the capital to debate the greatest of political problems: the need to launch the Republic properly and to make its actions vigorous and beneficial.

The government offers protection to the clubs. But so that their liberty, so that the Revolution itself should not be stopped short in its glorious progress, let us be wary, Citizens, of everything that can foster serious and enduring despondency in people's minds. Let it be recalled that this despondency nourishes counter-Revolutionary slanders and will strengthen the spirit of reaction. Let us therefore consider measures which, while ensuring public order, will put an end to alarmist rumour-mongering and calumny. If free discussion is a right, discussion backed by armed force is a threat. It may even become a form of tyranny. If the freedom of the clubs is one of the most inviolate victories gained by the Revolution, clubs whose members debate with arms in their hands can compromise liberty itself, excite conflict between passions, and lead to civil war.

Citizens, the provisional government, true to its principles, wishes for good order together with freedom of opinion. It has already taken appropriate measures to ensure the former.

Published in *Le Moniteur* of 20 April 1848, after a meeting on 19 April.

18 *The election campaign*

The documents in this section cast a great deal of light on social relationships. They reveal the continued existence of patron–client relationships, the dependence of the poor on those who provided work and charity, and leadership in the community. They also indicate that the dominance of the Notables in some places, in some situations, was being challenged by members of various social groups attempting to make use of a democratic constitution to constitute organized political groupings. Thus new social relationships were forming within the traditional society, as an effort was made to channel the energy generated by grievances into forms of sustained and more effective protest by means of institutionalized political dialogue.

INSTRUCTIONS TO DELEGATES OF THE CLUB OF CLUBS[1] (PARIS)
If the political adversary is noble, legitimist or monarchist, our delegate will stress the misfortunes that have been France's legacy from these monarchists and legitimists. They have always enriched themselves at the

[1] A grouping of delegates from various clubs and associations of workers created to co-ordinate electoral activity in the provinces.

workers' expense, oppressing the people, aiming to maintain privileges and heavy taxation. If the adversary is a financier, a man of wealth, the delegate will depict him as a man who has always taken from the farm-labourer, the peasant and the worker the major share of the profit from their work, discounting the sweat and toil of the people whom he oppressed even when the regime of self-interest was overthrown. . . .

In the cantons, communes and villages our delegate will encounter several forces: the parish priest, the schoolmaster, the justice of the peace, the tax collector, the lawyer; according to which profession it is, the tone should always be varied, though always tending to the Republican point of view. . . .

Thus, to the parish priest the delegate will cite, as the greatest prophet of Republicanism, Jesus Christ, who pronounced those divine words when tyranny and despotism were still strong everywhere: 'Walk ever in the ways of liberty, equality and fraternity, in the ways that lead to the pro-mised land.' As a priest of Jesus Christ he has a duty to preach Christian doctrine which is a doctrine of liberty, equality and fraternity.

To the schoolmaster he will always talk of freedom in education. He will emphasize all the benefits the Republic offers schoolmasters.

The tax collector, able to grant a respite to a taxpayer in difficulties and to stop him from being summonsed, exercises a definite influence. He is, it is true, a civil servant and accordingly should be well disposed. If he is not, he must be watched and reported to the Revolutionary committee.

As for the lawyer, he is afraid he may lose his job; he thinks he is ruined and is worried that privately validated contracts may replace contracts drawn up by lawyers. He must be reassured, and his hostility must be overcome. . . .

. . . with all the landowners, an effort must be made to reduce the bad effect produced by the measure increasing the tax by forty-five centimes. Say that the government is aware of the problems, and is thinking of going back on the measure, is thinking of charging a tax on mortgage debts, on luxuries, and that such a tax will be progressive. Insist on all these important points.

To sum up these instructions on the practical application of the manifesto, let us say that in a tactful, dignified and circumspect way, as well as with Republican zeal, the delegate must pay attention to all social classes, from the highest to the lowest. Taking into account habits and customs, he must modify his language and his conduct, in order to achieve the end in view – the election of Republican candidates.

See Archives nationales C.930.

ARTISANS AND FACTORY WORKERS

The workers are divided into two very large categories, those employed in factories and those belonging to the various artisan trades. The latter are very democratic and understand the proper meaning of the word 'liberty'. The former, on the other hand, mistake liberty for licence and are apt to commit disorders to avenge their suffering caused by their masters. Thus they are capable of compromising our cause.

Report (undated; of early April 1848) from Rouen of
M. Dahubert, delegate of the Club of Clubs (Archives
nationales C.940).

REPUBLICAN DIVISIONS

In this town there are two clubs that do not get on together. One is Republican but all its members are rich men; the other, popularly called the Black Club, is made up of workers.

Report from Gaillac (Tarn) of M. Rodier, delegate of the
Club of Clubs, 15 April 1848 (ibid.).

LINES OF CONFLICT

In complaining of various disturbances [the Procureur-général] blames the Comité démocratique of Rouen [as follows]: the committee is sending into this department, particularly into the Rouen area, agents whose task is the setting up and organizing of clubs and deputations who adopt a tone likely to provoke and stir up the working masses against the manufacturers and against the rich and the bourgeois in general.

From a report of the Procureur-général at Rouen, 4 April
1848 (ibid. BB[18] 1460).

Since I arrived in Rouen I have had conversations with quite a large number of inhabitants, especially from the commercial classes. . . . They are all enemies of anarchy and of the counter-Revolution. They wish to support the Republican government, but it must be a moderate Republic. The adjournment of the general elections has had a bad effect on the whole population of the area. It is the same in the Nord, Pas-de-Calais and Somme departments, which one of my political friends has toured recently. The delay in setting up the government is definitely considered the cause of the continually worsening commercial crisis which is crushing the country.

Report from Rouen by M. Cadiot, delegate of the Club
of Clubs, 12 April 1848 (Archives nationales C.940).

The bourgeoisie and the aristocracy make common cause with the clergy. They want to cause the defeat of the patriots and real Republicans at the elections.

Report (undated) from Dôle (Jura) by M. Guichard,
delegate of the Club of Clubs (ibid.).

In the country the most formidable influences are:
1. The clergy, who are false, jesuitical and two-faced; a party that cannot be distrusted too much.
2. The counter-Revolutionary party, *au juste milieu*; which is totally hostile to the Republic.
3. The Legitimist party; which is formidable on account of its alliance with the clergy.

Report from Quimper by M. Duval, delegate of the Club
of Clubs, 14 April 1848 (Archives nationales C.938).

EFFECTS OF THE FORTY-FIVE-CENTIME TAX

The decree relative to the forty-five-centime tax had, above all, a disastrous effect on the country folk. In the Charente, where the land is parcelled out in small lots and where the rural population itself owns most of the land, nearly everybody has been hit hard by this surtax.

The emissaries who came at election time and who went about the countryside preaching communistic and other socially subversive doctrines did more than strengthen a little the hand of the enemies of the Republic.

Report (undated) from the prefect of the Charente for the
*Rapport de la commission d'enquête sur l'insurrection qui a
éclate dans la journée du 23 juin sur les événements du 15 mai*
(commission of inquiry on the insurrection).

Everywhere the tax is having the worst possible effect on the Republican cause. Either they all refuse to pay up or else they simply cannot raise the money.

Report from the Jura by M. Mereaux, delegate of the
Club of Clubs (Archives nationales C.938).

That measure prevented the horrors of bankruptcy. But it was killing the Republic, for it made it hated in the countryside without making it any more popular in the towns.

Odilon Barrot, *Mémoires posthumes.*

FEAR OF COMMUNISM

Throughout Europe in the 1840s a 'Red Spectre' had arisen due to mounting social unrest caused by the social consequences of industrialization and harvest failures. Revolution seemed to confirm the worst fears. Subsequently, the evident power of the masses in the streets, the continued agitation in political clubs, newspapers and brochures, often extreme in promises and threats, and containing ritual obeisances to the Terror of 1793, served to heighten tension and exaggerate fears. Little violence in fact occurred before the June insurrection; in most regions there was a common desire to avoid it. Where traditional expressions of popular discontent did occur, they were at times believed to be inspired by communist ideas; but they were in fact short-lived outbursts, not steps in radical social reconstruction.

The rumour was put about that our delegate was going to preach female emancipation, St-Simonism and communism. He was pelted with stones and garbage.

Report from Vitré (Ille-et-Vilaine) by M. Peu, delegate of the Club of Clubs, 14 April 1848 (Archives nationales C.938).

Nobody appreciates the sublime virtues of abnegation and self-sacrifice. The bourgeois are scared by the phantom of communism and they terrify the ill-informed peasants by talking about it. The bankers and capitalists have ridiculous fears. . . . The worker himself seems for the most part not to be aware of the consequences of the solemn act he is about to perform. In Paris, people feel strong, happy and proud; in the provinces, it is as if people had leaden cloaks about their shoulders.

There are things about which it is best not to speak outside Paris. If you want to irritate the man you are talking to, lose his respect or perhaps expose yourself to a worse risk, mention the name of Robespierre or else introduce into your conversation the words communism, fourièrism, or even socialism.

Report from Ruffec (Charente) by M. Prat, delegate of the Club of Clubs, 10 April 1848 (ibid.).

1. . . . This town is dominated by proud aristocrats pretending to be Republicans, workers [who are] indifferent [and are] only wanting work, peasants full of prejudice, bourgeoisie looking up to the nobles.

Report from Alençon (Orne) by M. Stevenot, delegate of the Club of Clubs, 12 April 1848 (ibid. C.939).

The country folk in this area are completely under the thumb of the land-owners and will vote, if they vote at all, only under the influence of their lords and masters.

Report from Limoges by M. Lacoste, delegate of the Club of Clubs, 18 April 1848 (ibid. C.940).

The farther I go from the big cities the more I come across memories of the past and incomprehension of the present. . . . In Paris among those great enlightened people who overturned the government of vested interests it is appreciated that social inequality is a thing of the past. People hope for the future that was proclaimed by the man from Nazareth. In the principal towns of the various departments you also find noble, loyal hearts, spirits that foresee the future opened up for us by the coming of the Republic. But in the smaller places everything is different. The citizens are the victims of their own selfishness, or narrow-mindedness and of deplorable prejudices.

The bourgeoisie, nobles and money-grubbers, who yesterday were divided into many different camps, today make common cause in order to change the nature of the Revolution and to stem the tide of reform. . . . Workers who are still dependent on those people – and who feel it – do not dare lift up their heads. In public or in the clubs they protest only by their silence against the anti-liberal sentiments expressed by the aristocrats.

Report from Saint-Cloud (Charente) by M. Prat, delegate of the Club of Clubs, 13 April 1848 (ibid. C.938).

The people is not sufficiently educated to be able to make good use of its rights. It obeys old prejudices and paltry interests. It does not appreciate that great act it will perform the day after tomorrow. It will let itself be led along by the bourgeoisie. In consequence it is the bourgeoisie alone that will decide the elections. The workers and the peasants still tremble before their former lords and masters.

Ibid., report of 18 April 1848.

In Charente, the workers on the land, as in all the departments, far out-number the other inhabitants.

... Because of their ignorance, the bourgeoisie, the nobles and the clergy have maintained great influence over them. They will need to enjoy the exercise of Republican life for many years before they open their eyes. Accustomed to serve and obey, they are mistrustful on account of a few promises that have been made but not yet kept. When told that the era of abuse and privilege will utterly vanish, they reply by shaking their heads and saying: 'It's always been like this, and it always will be.'

Ibid., report of 7 May 1848.

The clergy have much influence. The bishop of Rouen has under his thumb eleven hundred priests who can each control twenty votes, *and* the clergy are Legitimist.

Report from Saint-Malo (Ille-et-Vilaine) by M. Deceau, delegate of the Club of Clubs, 10 April 1848 (ibid.).

Everything has still to be done in this area. People have not the slightest notion of Republicanism. All the officials have retained the positions they held under the former regime. The population does not understand how, in a Republic, you can possibly keep leaders who are incapable of rendering good service.

Report from Yssingeaux (Haute-Loire) by M. Mollin, delegate of the Club of Clubs, 12 April 1848 (ibid.).

In all communes nothing has been changed, with the result that the country folk think that, as in 1830, the government has only changed in name.

Report from the department of the Ain by M. Baciot, delegate of the Club of Clubs, 8 April 1848 (ibid. C.938).

In the countryside opinion is lukewarm, and in the *bocage*,[1] the clergy and the Legitimist party inspire fear and dread of the Republic. ... The authori-ties are lukewarm, make overtures only to the rich, and wish to see the assembly made up entirely of the well-to-do.

Report from Niort (Deux-Sèvres) by M. La Corbière, delegate of the Club of Clubs, 12 April 1848 (ibid.).

[1] 'The *bocage* is a landscape formed by hedge-enclosed fields, narrow, sunken roads, and dispersed villages, hamlets, and single farmsteads' (Charles Tilly).

The people are convinced that you have to be either rich or highly educated to be a deputy.

Report from the Haute-Marne by a delegate there of the
Club of Clubs, 9 April 1848 (ibid.).

The more I see of small towns and villages the better I understand the importance of education out in the countryside and the need to substitute new influences for old ones.

One of the means used by the reactionaries, bourgeoisie and clergy to win votes is to stir up animosity in the provinces against Paris. They say that Paris is not France, that it is no better to be subjugated to a city than to a king, and that what is needed is liberty, not dictatorship.

Report from the department of the Ain by M. Bouveyron,
delegate of the Club of Clubs, 17 April 1848 (ibid.).

19 The clergy and the elections

INSTRUCTIONS TO PARISH PRIESTS
We remind you of your obligation . . . to urge upon your parishioners the need to fulfil loyally their sacred duty as voters.

We know, dear colleague, the proper confidence they have in you. So help them with your good advice at this important juncture. Teach them how they should both select their candidate and exercise their voting rights. Overcome their objections. Sweep away their fears.

Take pains to explain to them that they are faced with the need to reconcile major interests and must banish all idea of party prejudice. They must concern themselves with one thing only, namely with choosing as their representatives men of recognized integrity who are frankly resolved to set up a Republic in France that respects the sacred rights of religion, liberty, property and the family. . . .

Finally, dearly beloved colleague, set your parishioners a good example. Go to the polls at the head of your congregation.

The bishop of Rennes in a circular letter addressed to the
clergy of his diocese (ibid. C.941).

INFLUENCE OF THE CLERGY
The clergy of the Tarn department in general, with very few exceptions, behaved throughout the elections as the enemies of the Republic. Though they declared publicly that they were loyal supporters of the February

Revolution, they worked to the best of their ability to ensure the election of its adversaries.

In the Tarn department the Catholic clergy always march with the Legitimist party. With the elections at hand they formed a committee called the 'Religious Committee'. The Legitimists nominated the candidates, the priests endorsed them, and it was remarkable how they all worked energetically together.

Sermons from the pulpit, advice, homilies, commands, threats uttered in the homes and in the confessionals, pressure brought to bear on the electors' relations, harangues – some pronounced in public, some otherwise –slanders, lies about the Republican candidates, whom they represented as communists, terrorists and enemies of religion. . . .

Report of the government commissaire in the Tarn to the minister of public worship, 28 May 1848 (ibid. F^{19} 5604).

0 Popular indifference

The spirit in the department is one of total indifference to political matters. There is little concern about the form or the nature of the central government. Local customs are supported and, for many years now, the department has been subject to personal influences. Those who wield them wish to continue to do so, and the new men wish to inherit this influence so they too can benefit in their turn. So, when the Republic came into being, it won almost unanimous acceptance. At the time of the elections, there was a purely local struggle for position.

Report (undated; of June 1848) by the prefect of the Basses-Pyrénées to the commission of inquiry on the insurrection.

1 Weakness of the Republican electoral campaign

There have been more mischievous revolutionaries than those of 1848, but I doubt if there have been any more stupid. They knew neither how to make use of universal suffrage nor how to manage without it. . . .

Following examples from the past without understanding them, they gullibly imagined that to summon the people to political life was enough to attach them to their cause; and that if they gave the people rights but no advantages, it was enough to make the Republic popular. They forgot that their predecessors, when they gave every peasant a vote, at the same time did away with tithes, abolished the *corvée* and other seignoral privileges, and divided the nobles' land among their former serfs; however, there was nothing similar that they could do. By establishing universal suffrage they thought they were summoning the people to support the Revolution, whereas they were only arming them against it. I am, however, far from believing that it was impossible for Revolutionary passions to have been roused even in the country districts. In France every farmer owns some part of the soil, and most of their smallholdings are encumbered with debt; therefore, the creditor rather than the noble was their enemy, and it was he who should have been attacked. Not the abolition of property rights, but the abolition of debts should have been promised.

Alexis de Tocqueville, *Recollections*.

22 *The election*

This was the first election to be held with universal male suffrage. The lack of experience and of independence of much of the electorate made it inevitable that conservative Notables should exert a considerable influence. Political structures were fluid. There were no organized political parties as we know them, but rather groupings of candidates of similar tendency selected by local committees, often with informal links with Parisian committees which supplied advice and propaganda material. Almost all candidates pledged allegiance to the Republic, most also to the defence of the existing social order, and, in addition, to doing something for the poor. It is not easy, consequently, to distinguish political tendencies and to interpret the results. For ideological reasons, government interference in the campaign was far less than it ever had been or would be for many decades. In that respect this was a 'free' election, but, in adopting a neutral stance, the provisional government left the field open for conservative notables to reassert their predominant influence, in many places virtually unchallenged.

To prevent the people being deceived, the club, at my suggestion, split up into several sections, and, with a standard bearer at their head, they went out on to the roads to wait for the peasants coming in to vote. For the most part these were led by landowners and tenant farmers who hoped to make them behave like so many silly sheep and waste their opportunity.

. . . Every time a commune arrived, the club members fraternized with the peasants, inquiring about their voting intentions and asking whether they were in favour of the counter-Revolution. They tried to make them understand and substituted for their lists the names of candidates adopted by the delegates of the twenty-six cantons.

Report from Moulins (Allier) by M. Famberta, delegate
of the Club of Clubs, 25 April 1848 (Archives nationales
C.938).

Universal suffrage. Leading politicians watch anxiously as the nation votes.

3 Election results

The abolition of property qualification [for voting], which meant that some of the electors were dependent on the rich, and the visible changes threatening property, which made people choose those who had the most interest in defending it, were the main reasons for the presence [in parliament] of the great number of landowners. The election of the ecclesiastics was due to similar reasons, and also to . . . the very widespread and quite unexpected return of a great part of the nation to a concern with religious matters.

When the Revolution of '92 struck the upper classes, it cured them of their lack of religion; it vividly taught them, if not the truth, at least the social usefulness of belief. . . . the Revolution of 1848 had done for the bourgeoisie just what '92 had done for the nobility. . . .

Alexis de Tocqueville, *Recollections.*

24 Election results and reactions to them

We must not hide anything from ourselves: the elections are going against the men who worked for the Republic and proclaimed it. The first step is an attack on us, to be followed by an assault on our principles.

From *La Réforme*, 1 May 1848.

There is no longer any doubt about the outcome of the election. You would have to be blind or an enemy of the people not to agree that the alliance of all the privileged classes is triumphing over the People.

It is certain that the bourgeoisie will be masters of the national assembly. The People should have no more illusions about this.

So the role of the popular Republicans is fatally settled. After bringing about the Revolution two months ago, here we are again, as before, condemned to fight. We shall not be the opposition, as they used to call that collection of comedians and place-seekers who used to play out their part and go along with Orléanist groups. We shall represent the future. We shall not be content just to block measures. We shall be the active and loyal soldiers who will lead forward all the friends of the social Republic. . . .

The various elements making up the national assembly will all come together, we can foresee, on one capital issue – the blocking of social reform. This thing called a Republic will be organized, with the prime object of resisting all popular demands.

From *La Vraie République*, 30 April 1848.

Club of the National Mobile Guard.
QUESTION   What would be the duty of the citizens if the national assembly were to get bogged down, and make no progress and did not extirpate every abuse?
REPLY (*unanimous*)   An uprising.

Club de la Garde nationale mobile Paris, minutes of the meeting of 5 April 1848 (Archives nationales C.930).

25 Paris at the end of April 1848

In that city there were a hundred thousand armed workmen formed into regiments, without work and dying of hunger. Society was cut in two: those who had nothing united in common envy; those who had anything united in common terror. There were no longer ties of sympathy linking these two great classes, and a struggle was everywhere assumed to be inevitable soon. . . .

A dull despair had descended on the oppressed and threatened middle classes, but imperceptibly that despair was turning into courage. I had always thought that there was no hope of gradually and peacefully controlling the impetus of the February Revolution and that it could only be stopped suddenly by a great battle taking place in Paris. . . . What I now saw persuaded me that the battle was not only inevitable but imminent, and that it would be desirable to seize the first opportunity to start it.

Alexis de Tocqueville, *Recollections*.

6 The Left organizes

Excitement and hostility are still at a high pitch in the political groups. The possibility of rebellion is still considered as serious, imminent and inevitable. The clubs have reached no decision about an armed uprising. But the Central Club for the Rights of Man has resolved to use all possible means to summon the people out on to the streets in order to bring pressure on the representatives. It is plain that they have not the confidence to start a battle. But their aim is to organize things in such a way that they will be maltreated by the national guard. Then they will have a good justification for defending themselves – and for attacking in their turn.

Report of the Paris prefect of police, 3 May 1848 (Archives nationales C.930).

7 Republicans and the constituent assembly[1]

THE ATTITUDES OF REVOLUTIONARIES

These men of bad faith forget their origins too quickly. Woe to them if they already think they are strong enough to crush the people, their sovereign masters. The constituent assembly is nothing other than a *national workshop*, the group of workers called on by the nation to work on its account. The day when these workers fail to satisfy their masters, they can be thrown out of the workshop and be replaced by more faithful servants.

Société républicaine centrale, minutes of the meeting of 9 May 1848 (Archives nationales C.930).

[1] The assembly met for the first time on 4 May 1848. This document illustrates the speed at which the political situation deteriorated.

Again, if only they hid their tendencies! But these new democrats have only one thought in their heads, that of pushing the Republicans aside, so far as that is possible. . . . For them every innovation will be a danger, every modification of the social structure so much pillaging. . . .

No, there has been no revolution; that must be said again. It is a compromise they claim we must agree to, that is all. Equal rights is, once again, just a form of words.

From *La Réforme*, 12 May 1848.

28 Government preparations to suppress disorder

The council determines . . . that the minister of war be authorized to order the return to Paris of five regiments, three of infantry and two of cavalry. Citizen Albert voted against this resolution and asked that his opposition be recorded in the minutes.

Government decision of 21 April 1848; not published in *Le Moniteur*. Cited in C. H. Pouthas (ed.), *Procès-verbaux du Gouvernement provisoire et de la Commission du pouvoir executif*, Paris 1950.

29 The demonstration of 15 May 1848

THE CONSERVATIVE VIEW
To dominate the assembly, just as the convention had been dominated by the sections, or to get rid of it by forcing it to disperse – that was the dream of the clubs.

Charles de Rémusat, *Mémoires*.

MODERATE REPUBLICAN FEAR OF REVOLUTION
One part of the populace, giving rein to most noble sentiments, associated itself with a demonstration in support of Poland. Under the cover of the demonstration a plot was being mounted against the assembly, against the whole nation, whose life, essence, thought, and energy is expressed by the assembly, in fact against the Republic itself. The sovereignty of the people itself has been attacked in this attack upon its representatives.

From *Le National*, 16 May 1848.

[On 15 May] they had not . . . any premeditated plan of action. There were more than a hundred different institutes in the procession, each with its own banner and its own leaders, who would act according to their own view of the case, and according to circumstances; they were, however, so far agreed that they wished to impart a democratic impulse to the chamber, which had already betrayed its reactionary tendencies.

L. M. Caussidière, *Mémoires.*

THE LEFT DIVIDED IN ITS INTENTIONS

There has been something very odd at the Blanqui club these last few days. It is that M. Blanqui himself has discovered that he has been overtaken by some of his supporters. One of the speakers demanded that the people should take action immediately· But the president of the club, M. Blanqui himself, has spoken out against him two days running, declaring that it would be imprudent to embark on matters in so hasty and drastic a fashion, that the working masses have so far no firm principles, and that by trying to press on so fast there was a risk of bringing everything into jeopardy.

Report from the Paris correspondent of *La Liberté* in Rouen; 17 May 1848.

GROWING CONSERVATIVE FEARS

The Polish matter was only a pretext for the demonstration that had been announced. The real plan was to dissolve the national assembly by force and bring us back to that reign of bloody terror which, fifty-five years ago, covered France with gibbets and victims.

Ibid.

From the depths of my retreat [a château in Aude] I read the newspapers avidly. I thanked Heaven for the recent delivery of France from one of the greatest risks it had ever run. . . . Had Barbès succeeded, a Revolutionary committee would inevitably have been set up instead of the constituent assembly, and soon the whole land would have been plunged in mourning. Those people would have gone beyond even the horrors of '93. In their view, the guillotine did not do its work fast enough. In every village in France they would have proclaimed the need to kill us all in our homes.

General Marquis Alphonse d'Hautpoul, *Mémoires.*

30 Demands for a showdown

The national guard is ready to take energetic action. All the citizens who have industrial or commercial interests prefer a violent confrontation to letting things drag on, which undermines them even more certainly. There are complaints that the government lacks vigour. It is said that, when faced with all the various abuses resulting from the national workshops, the government should have taken decisive steps. The national guard would have given its wholehearted support.

Report of the Paris prefect of police, 29 May 1848
(Archives nationales C.930).

31 Agitation and organization in Paris

I have carefully noted the nature of these gatherings seen in the street over the last fortnight, of the speeches made by the ringleaders, and the fact that the manufacturers can neither get the workers back into their workshops, where there is employment for them, nor even keep those who had remained.[1] This has led me to the conviction that a hostile organization is behind these disorders. The alliance is organized by the delegates to the Luxembourg.

The delegates to the Luxembourg are represented by an executive committee. Besides this supreme executive council, which represents the combined interests of all the industries, each section has its own committee which arranges for the supreme committee's decrees to be carried out.

Report of the Paris prefect of police, 3 June 1848 (ibid.).

32 Strikers in Paris

[Six employers] . . . refused to accept the wage rates put forward by the workers. Thus they have not been able to complete the various orders received over the last three months. . . . The workers were employed in the national workshops, and they also received five francs a week extra from the chapel's fund, which has been in existence for twenty-five years and has reserves.

Letter from the Comité spécial des Chapeliers (Hatters),
presented as evidence to the commission of inquiry on the
insurrection.

[1] Employment in the national workshops strengthened the position of strikers.

3 National workshops

THE GOVERNMENT VIEW

The national workshops, their numbers swollen by poverty and laziness, became every day a heavier burden, a less productive element in society and a greater menace to public order. They were only a makeshift to ensure good order and to provide a primitive form of public relief for the poor, which became necessary in the days following the Revolution, when the people had to be fed. And it had not been merely a question of feeding them; they had to be kept busy, too, if disorder was not to result from their unemployment.

Alphonse de Lamartine, *Histoire de la révolution de 1848.*

THE CONSERVATIVE VIEW

The national workshops – set up not as casual places of shelter, but as the permanent refuges which society owes to the unemployed – allowed the workers to demand from the masters inflated wages. The worker, protected by the state against the ill-effects of unemployment, could put the master out of business by his demands, and there was almost no way of avoiding that.

Hostile comment on productivity in the national workshops.

... The national workshops received a growing population. The men were supported during their strikes by the government, which paid them for doing nothing. They were encouraged by speeches that were hostile to the masters. The men's solidarity in their strikes was confirmed, and they became more and more hostile to the employers. As this system developed the alarm increased in industry and commerce. The workers' poverty helped swell what the employers regarded as the army of anarchy.

From *Le Constitutionnel*, 22 June 1848.

The maintaining of national workshops offered temptations to idleness which it was necessary to get rid of. These workshops had been represented, immediately after the February Revolution, as a provisional resource imposed by imperious necessity. [But] we found ourselves ... faced by an agglomeration of a hundred thousand ... paid by the state for fictitious work, and become, clandestinely at first, openly afterward, a dangerous army of socialism. To bring the evil to light and to endeavour to remedy it seemed to the Labour committee the first thing they had to do.

Count de Falloux[1], *Mémoires*.

DECISION TO RUN THEM DOWN
At Citizen Garnier-Pagès' proposal, the commission resolves that the registers of workers for the national workshops shall be closed; that lists shall be opened for workers aged between eighteen and twenty-five years who are willing to sign on for an engagement in the army. Those who refuse to do so will be sent back to their home districts.

Decision of the executive commission of the government,
13 May 1848; not published in *Le Moniteur* until 22 June.
(Restrictions on entry into the national workshops,
however, started immediately.)

The Commission decides on the following measures relative to the national workshops:
All the workers who have been in Paris for less than six months are to be sent away from the capital with marching orders. . . .

[1] Falloux was a leading member of the constituent assembly's committee on labour.

Labour exchanges are to be opened where employers will be able to come and ask for workers. Those workers who refuse jobs in particular industries will immediately be sent away from the national workshops.

Decision of the executive commission of the government, 23 May 1848; not published in *Le Moniteur* until 4 June.

The commission of executive power decides that, within five days, the workers in the national workshops aged between eighteen and twenty-five must accept a two-year engagement in the army or, if they refuse, be excluded from the workshops.

Decision of the executive commission of the government, 16 June 1848; published in *Le Moniteur* 22 June.

THE MEASURES SEEN AS PROVOCATIVE

. . . More effort could have been made, in our view, to prepare opinion for the announcement; more prudence could have been shown. Because the announcement was sudden and because there was a lack of reassuring comment, there is a danger of jeopardizing this decision which has been staved off for so long.

It is plain that the assistance provided for the workers will be cut off only when they have found alternative means of livelihood. Doubtless the government has other measures up its sleeve. It should have announced them, or, at least, have given some hint. It is regrettable that these precautions were not taken to allay all the workers' anxieties about this and to avoid creating alarm.

This new decision by the government could not have been presented in a more unfortunate fashion, and indeed there are already reports of disquiet in the national workshops.

From *Le Constitutionnel*, 23 June 1848.

WORKERS' REACTIONS TO THE THREATENED CLOSURES

Addressed to Minister Goudchaux: 'Are you really the man who was the first finance minister of the Republic, of the Republic won at the cost of blood thanks to the workers' courage, of this Republic whose first vow was to provide bread every day for all its children by proclaiming the universal right to work? Work, who will give it to us if not the state at a time when industry has everywhere closed its workshops, shops and factories? Yesterday martyrs for the Republic out on the barricades, today its defenders in the ranks of the national guard, the workers might consider it owed them something. . . .

'Why do the national workshops so rouse your reprobation . . .? You are not asking for their reform, but for their total abolition. But what is to be done with this mass of 110,000 workers who are waiting each day for their modest pay, for the means of existence for themselves and their families? Are they to be left a prey to the evil influences of hunger and of the excesses that follow in the wake of despair?'

Poster signed *Les membres du bureau provisoire du Club de l'Union des Brigadiers des Ateliers nationaux*; dated 20 June 1848 (Archives nationales C.930).

We are not people asking for charity. The Republic promised work to provide a livelihood for all its children. . . . So give us work so that we may live like free men. . . .

Do not forget, Monarchists, that it was not so that we could remain your slaves that we brought about a third revolution. We fought your social system, the sole cause of the disorder and poverty that devours and swallows contemporary society.

Réponse des Ouvriers à Dupin: signed by the workers of the 19th brigade of the national workshops; undated (ibid.).

I live in the faubourg; by trade I am a cabinet-maker and I am enrolled in the national workshops, waiting for trade to pick up again.

I went into the workshops when I could no longer find bread elsewhere. Since then people have said we were given charity there. But when I went in I did not think that I was becoming a beggar. I believed that my brothers who were rich were giving me a little of what they had to spare simply because I was their brother.

I admit that I have not worked very hard in the national workshops, but then I have done what I could. I am too old now to change my trade easily – that is one explanation. But there is another: the fact is that, in the national workshops, there was absolutely nothing to do.

Letter to the editor of the newspaper *L'Aimable Fabourien*, appearing in the issue of 4 June 1848 (ibid.).

4 A symptom of discontent: Bonapartism

We are informed that the popularity of Citizen Louis Bonaparte seems to be rising rapidly. His name is very often on the workers' lips. Many say he should be made head of the Republic.

Report of the Paris prefect of police, 4 June 1848 (ibid.).

5 Murmurs of insurrection

Report of the discussion among a group of workers near the Place de la Bastille early in June: There was talk of the poverty of the workers in the faubourg St-Antoine and of contempt for the executive commission. Some people said that Prince Napoléon ought to be backed up. But the question they returned to again and again was the question of armed conflict to overthrow the assembly. One man there . . . was talking socialism. He was a workman, and exerted some authority over the various groups. 'The mistake the people made in February,' he said, 'and the one we must be on guard against this time, was this: we didn't nominate our deputies out there on the actual barricades. But it's there you must nominate them, for it is there we see them at work. Yes, we must get rid of the aristos. Lamartine is a White and an aristo. Why are Albert and Barbès at Vincennes?[1] Any constitution drawn up in their absence is sure to be bad.'

He seemed, however, to have more balanced views when he spoke of trade and industry. He thought that advancing money to the leaders of industry would really be more beneficial to the workers than poor relief, even if it was earned in the national workshops. He kept on making this point in different ways. He was well received and listened to carefully.

[They were] assured that the mobile guard[2] was and always would be behind the workers. . . . All these people admitted they had muskets and ammunition in their possession . . . that the bourgeois guard would not fight, that it was scared, and that the regulars had had enough and still remembered February.

. . . The workers always ended up by saying, 'There have been rich people for too long. They own everything and are heartless. They just laugh at us. It's time we stopped being poor.'

Many stated that they sometimes did not have anything to eat, and they had many children. They painted grim pictures of their home life.

Letter from a professor at the École centrale (presented as evidence to the commission of inquiry on the insurrection).

[1] Imprisoned there following the demonstration of 15 May.

[2] Recruited primarily from young unemployed workers.

What we have to say to you is this. Liberty, equality and fraternity are at risk and a frightful struggle may be joined in the name of this sacred motto for the sake of which you have twice endured martyrdom.

The reaction against which you spoke a few days ago . . . grows in strength hour by hour. The Republic of Privilege, purblind handmaiden of royalty, rears up, threatening to block the road along which for three score years democracy has striven to advance by means of words, the pen, and the sword.

A new social crisis is at hand: responsibility for it will fall on those who have provoked it. Thanks to the stupidity of some and the ill-will of others, that February victory which should, from the humanitarian viewpoint have been the glorious culmination of our fathers' labours will perhaps only be recalled in history as a passing breeze in the interval between two storms.

Address voted by the Club de la Révolution to A. Barbès,
its president; published in *La Presse*, 19 June 1848.
(Barbès had been imprisoned after the demonstration of
15 May.)

Part Two:
The June Insurrection

The government decision to run down the national workshops was the occasion for conflict but not altogether the cause of it. The workshops symbolized the popular victory of February and all the hopes of the Parisian poor. The threat to them was a threat to aspirations toward a better life. To Conservatives the workshops represented the Revolution organized, and had to be eliminated. The actual struggle was confused, the forces of order including many committed Republicans who put defence of the Republic before further social reform. Thus workers fought on both sides. Of crucial importance was the fact that on this occasion, especially when compared with February, the government was determined to crush insurrection, and supplied clear directives to the military forces organized for this purpose.

1 The beginnings of insurrection

Thursday, 22 June 1848

10.45 A.M.   Two hundred and fifty to three hundred people, following banners emblazoned with the words 'National Workshops', crossed the Tuileries palace bridge, crossed the Quai des Tuileries and the Place du Carousel. They proceeded via the Rue Saint-Honoré towards the Place du Palais National. They were singing the *Chant du Départ*. As they passed in front of the barracks where the mobile guard were quartered, they shouted 'Up with the Mobiles!'

11.00 A.M.   A column of five hundred people, headed by a banner, has just marched through the 7th *arrondissement*. The men in it say they will not go away to Sologne[1] and that they prefer to die here. They add that they will take up arms against the national assembly, and that the mobile guard will support them.

The same group, as it went along the Rue Saint-Honoré, shouted 'Napoléon forever! We won't go!'

NOON   There are two quite large groups at the Hôtel-de-Ville. There is a lot of talk there about Sologne. They say that the region is unhealthy, that the workers should refuse to go, and that the government has taken this step only in order to get rid of them.

The column in question proceeded into the Rue du faubourg Saint-

---

[1] Work was to be provided draining marshes there.

Antoine. The people in it chanted again and again: 'We won't go!' They shouted furious insults about citizens Lamartine and Marie, saying that the rich are thieves. They said too that this evening at six they are all going to gather at the Pantheon.

5.00 P.M. The workers have started to arrive. A group of six to seven hundred people, mostly in overalls, swarmed over the Place du Pantheon shouting various slogans.

7.00 P.M. Some four or five thousand workers are standing waiting now on the Place du Pantheon and in the immediate vicinity. This tumultuous and excited mob suddenly starts to break up. A powerful column of workers goes off towards the faubourg Saint-Marcel. They say they are going to join their friends from the faubourg Saint-Antoine.

Another goes down the Rue Saint-Jacques and seems to be making its way towards the Hôtel-de-Ville.

7.15 P.M. This column is composed of around three thousand workers from the markets and is headed by a dozen national workshop banners. It crosses the Rue de la Cité, the Notre-Dame Bridge, and goes into the Rue Saint-Martin shouting 'Work! Work! Bread! We won't go!' Others shout, 'We'll get it, we'll get it!' A few shout 'Barbès forever!'

7.45 P.M. The crowd which has passed right along the Rue Saint-Martin turns into the Boulevard Saint-Martin and goes off toward the Place de la Bastille. Some eight or nine hundred persons swell the column as it goes on its way.

9.00 P.M. A column whose strength may be estimated at between eight and ten thousand persons, and which appears to come from the faubourg Saint-Antoine, is passing at this moment in front of the Hôtel-de-Ville. This mass, in the midst of which a great number of banners can be seen, is making its way toward the Pantheon, in order to join forces with the workers of the 12th *arrondissement*. Various shouts emanate from this crowd which also includes women. They demand work and they add 'We won't go! We'll get him! We'll hang him! The Republic for ever!' Some want massacre and looting, shouting 'Down with traitors! Down with the national guard! It's got to stop!'

9. 30 P.M. The crowd goes up the Rue Saint-Jacques, headed by a hundred urchins with candles in their hands and shouting 'Barbès forever!' or 'Put a bullet in them!' The shops close as this column passes on its way to the Place du Pantheon.

10.00 P.M. It is taken as certain that the workers meeting at the Place du Pantheon are arranging to meet tomorrow and that they are talking of barricades.

11.00 P.M.   The meeting has broken up of its own accord, and the Place du Pantheon is entirely empty.

Report of the Paris prefect of police, 22 June 1848;
presented as evidence to the commission of inquiry on the
insurrection.

2 Military tactics

Had we had the smallest forces available on Friday, by 2 p.m. we would have prevented the erection of the barricades. The national guard, seeing no troops arriving, became demoralized, and most went off home. The rebels were hesitating: work on the large barricade dismantled on Friday night by the regulars and the national guard did not begin again until five o'clock the next morning. . . . On Saturday great masses joined in with the insurgents because it seemed certain they would be successful. There was absolutely no fanaticism in general, except on the part of a few individuals. A certain number of women, too, became very excited; but passions were far from being generally raised.

Deposition of M. Joubert, director of the Paris customs
posts, to the commission of inquiry on the insurrection.

3 Barricades in Paris

The total number of barricades of all descriptions in the parts of the city where this reconnaissance took place amounts to two hundred and fifty. Those constructed of planks or barrels are exceptional. Nearly all have foundations made up of paving stones, though the quantity used varies.

. . . Everywhere the paving stones have been dug up and piled on a strip of roadway which has been left intact. The width of the strip varies between 1·5 and 3, 4 or 5 metres. The height is very variable. The widest, which are 3 or 4 metres high, are in the Vielle Rue du Temple and in the Rues Saint-Martin, Aumaire and Rambuteau.

. . . An important feature is the communications system between various roads which the rebels have established across houses, gardens and open land in several parts of the city, especially in the faubourg du Temple. Thus they could, for example, go from one barricade to another in this suburb and in the Rue Fontaine-au-Roi without exposing themselves to the fire of the troops attacking them.

Report of a military reconnaissance (Archives historiques
du Ministère de la Guerre, Mémoires historiques no. 902).

4 The course of insurrection

On 24 June, at 3 a.m., the insurgents knocked on all the doors, especially those of the workers, forcing residents to accompany them to the barricades. Around 9 a.m., several came to parley at the barracks. They asked for arms and ammunition to be handed over to them, promising not to attack the soldiers. Captain Corbuet declined to give them anything. They made preparations to attack. They demanded that doors opening on to the street should not be closed, presumably so that they would be able to take shelter if need be and so that they could shoot from behind cover. They set fire to the barracks gate with bales of straw and hay, sprayed with petrol, and stacks of barrel hoops stolen from my premises. When the door was burnt down they could not get in because the captain had put up behind it a makeshift barricade of iron bedsteads. Then they decided to set fire to my house, hoping to bring crashing down a portion of the parti-wall between it and the barracks. . . . But the wall remained standing.

Deposition of M. Justin-Henri Coffin, brewer, of 11 Rue
de Reuilly, to the commission of inquiry on the
insurrection.

5 Reasons for insurrection

Some of the foremen and the delegates of the national workshops tried by every possible means to stop us going off to the provinces. They urged on us the need to stand firm against the first attack.

Deposition of M. Jarry, worker in the national workshops,
to the commission of the inquiry on the insurrection.

Q. To what end did you go to build the barricade on which you were arrested?
R. It had already been started when we got there. We built it because they wanted to send the workers away from Paris. We did not mean any harm. We thought it was just like it had been in February.

From proceedings of the second court martial: the trial of
Louis Bosquet, hatter; reported in *Le National*,
7 September 1848.

ACCUSED   Hearing the re-call I went out with my musket. They gave me some drinks and led me to the barricade blocking the way. There they said to me 'Look, are you going to shoot?' 'Hell', I said, 'who at?' 'Are you going to shoot?' they repeated, 'If not, you'll have to hand over your musket.' And they took it away. The next day they made me take one from a wounded man. . . . I only fired twice.

Q.   Why did you agree to fire?

R.   I was carried away, like lots of others. The ones who wouldn't go along with them got called idlers and were maltreated.

Q.   But did you not know that when you fired on Paris you were firing on your brothers?

R.   Yes. But they told us it wasn't the same thing. A man like me up from the country, who had never heard these things talked about, had never seen anything, and who couldn't read or write – a man like me is easily led astray.

From proceedings of the second court martial: the trial of
M. Brichet, labourer, employed by the Northern Railway
Company; reported in *Le National*, 7 September 1848.

An insurgent leader at the Barrières de Charenton . . . gave as the reason for the revolt the desire for a democratic and social republic. I asked him to explain what he meant by social; he replied . . . the right of workers to form associations and to take part, according to their ability, in public and private enterprises.

From the report of the officer commanding the 1st
battalion of the 4th legion of the national guard of the
banlieu (Archives historiques du Ministère de la Guerre
$F^1 9$).

ACCUSED   Citizens, the Republic has always been my only idea, my only dream. Twice I have been thrown into gaol for working for the setting up of the democratic Republic. . . .

Q.   What do you mean by a social Republic?

R.   I mean a Republic with social reforms. Universal suffrage has been decreed, but that doesn't do the people any good. It is an instrument that the people do not use, that they do not know how to use. I want free and compulsory education for all and the organization of work through association; finally I want to ensure that the worker receives the product of his labour, a proportion of which is at present taken away from him by the man who provides the capital. Then there would be no poverty, and so there would be no Revolution to fear. If the authorities had done that instead of fruitlessly spending vast sums on the national workshops there would not have been an uprising in June. The workers enrolled in the national workshops would rather have done proper work than received money for doing nothing.

From proceedings of the second court martial: the trial of
Louis-Auguste Raccari, engineering worker; reported in
Le National, 27 August 1848.

The worker did not take up arms because of his own sufferings. He did so because he felt for his old father, his wife, his children and his workmates. He protested against the prolongation of poverty, not just because it is torture to the body, but because it is oppression to the soul.

Louis Blanc, *Révélations historiques*.

6 *Sympathetic response in the provinces*

The Corbeil national guard has been in Paris. During its absence the factory workers in Essonne and its environs have built a barricade here, with the object of preventing the passage of troops on their way from Fontainbleau to Paris. The Essonne national guard refused to assist in dismantling this barricade.

Report on the five-day period 20–25 June 1848 by the
general officer commanding the 1st military division
(Archives historiques du Ministère de la Guerre F^1 16).

At Amiens, our working classes were already becoming inflamed. I myself heard people saying: 'It's not a question of the Republic. It's a question of conflict between masters and workers. We ought to go and fight for the workers against the masters.' These words reveal, only too clearly I fear, the true meaning of this war and the danger of the present situation.

From a report by the Procureur-général at Amiens,
25 July 1848 (Archives nationales BB^{18} 1465).

7 *Fear in the provinces*

Insurrection completely put down. All rebels have laid down arms or are running away across the countryside.

Telegraphed dispatch of 26 June 1848 from General
Cavaignac, head of government, to generals commanding
military divisions, and to prefects and sub-prefects
(Archives historiques du Ministère de la Guerre F^1 9).

The town of Châlons was in a state of great unrest yesterday. There were false reports that the town of Épernay was burning and awash with blood and that looting was taking place.

. . . The villagers were armed with scythes, pick-axes, anything that they might defend themselves with. In Châlons it was said that Épernay was being pillaged, and the same was being said about Châlons in Reims.

Report from Châlons of 29 June 1848 by the officer
commanding the 3rd subdivision of the 3rd military
division (ibid.).

A crowd gathered for a sale: . . . These people were heard and seen in the distance. This gave rise to the notion that it was a mob of insurgents fleeing from Paris. Fear immediately spread over all the neighbouring communes. Soon everything became so exaggerated that every village thought it was threatened with burning and looting.

Report by the Procureur de la République at Domfront
(Orne), 5 July 1848 (Archives nationales BB^{30} 359).

8 *In defence of society*

Many detachments of volunteers were formed at the first call to march on Paris. . . . Under these circumstances, the various parties not wishing to see the overthrow of all social order said nothing for a while about their disagreements. They wished only to go to the aid of society, whose very existence they judged threatened by a horde of barbarians. Young men known to belong to the Legitimist party were noted among the keenest in the ranks of volunteers in the national guard, either because being men of leisure they had less difficulty in getting away in a hurry, or else because being rich, for the most part, they had a livelier sense of the grave threat posed to property.

From a report by the Procureur-général at Angers,
5 July 1848; presented as evidence to the commission of
inquiry on the insurrection.

Known Legitimists and Orléanists . . . were very keen to persuade the national guard to go and fight the insurgents. All the same, they took pains to explain that it was not on behalf of the Republic that they were doing this, for they had no respect for it. Their concern was purely with the preservation and maintenance of order.

From a report of the Procureur-général at Caen, 4 July
1848; presented as evidence to the commission of inquiry
on the insurrection.

9 The brutality of repression

At 8.30 a.m. two men tried to escape as the cells were being reallocated. They were killed and immediately thrown into the Seine.

. . . Today at 5 a.m. two detainees who were attempting to escape after forcing a lock were immediately killed.

From a report of the general commanding the Place de
Paris, 28 June 1848 (Archives historiques du Ministère
de la Guerre F[1] 9).

10 Marseilles: demonstration of 22 June

Many workers had refused to go there. Those employed at M. Taylor's factory in particular had resisted every endeavour to win their support. These workers, numbering some five hundred, all received wages high enough to make them content with their conditions and anxious about the maintenance of order. . . .

Having regard to the fact that these serious confrontations in Marseille coincided with the bloody days of rioting in Paris, it was impossible not to wonder whether the men responsible for these two uprisings had not agreed in advance on plans to act together. . . . Reports have revealed several circumstances that lead naturally to suspicions of a plot. The arrival at Marseilles of men from Lyon and Paris who were members of the Italian Legion,[1] the speeches supporting the events of 15 May and defending Barbès, which they declaimed in the clubs, the presence of a large number of them in rowdy demonstrations. . . .

A Republican magistrate knows the respect due to the liberty of opinion. He will have every sympathy for all the various sorts of suffering. But he detects and condemns every violent attack on social order. A defender of public peace, property and the family, he knows his duties and will know how to match his unshakeable devotion to duty with the major interests of society.

Report (undated) of the Procureur-général at Aix
(Archives nationales BB[18] 1465).

[1] Formed to create a united Italy.

1 Conservative explanation of the June insurrection

The Luxembourg palace theories have been disastrous. They gave birth to hopes that could not be satisfied. When the national assembly came together and was unable to cope with demands far in excess of everybody's desire and beyond all possibility of fulfilment, people attacked it violently. . . . [This] was a consequence of that sort of utopianism.

The turmoil in certain clubs produced civil war. It is on their heads that the blood that has been shed should fall now. The strength of the rebellion lay no doubt in the poverty of many of the insurgents. But if it was possible for base agitators to exploit this suffering which was, alas, only too real, the determining factor in all these plots is found in subversive theories and in wild and reckless ambition.

Another proof that the rebellion was not spontaneous – that is, not simply a sudden reaction to hunger – is that it is so well organized. It has its own regulations, its leaders and its meeting-places. It has many ramifications in the departments and links with all the forces for disorder, and it operates with heart-breaking confidence and astonishing efficiency.

Report of the commission of inquiry on the insurrection.

The character of the February Revolution – its ease, speed and consequences, the hopes and desires it had given rise to among the masses, the prejudices it had produced or confirmed in their minds, the doctrines that had been ascribed to them, the promises that had been made, the rights that had been allowed to them, the powers they had been given – this unheard-of example of the working-class population of a great capital city in one of the most industrialized societies being granted not only political power, but having it in fact and as of right – and all that made yet worse by the discredit or·disappearance of most of the influences and the structures of political order, by the cessation of virtually all paid work, by the intense, endless unemployment and by poverty – all this inevitably led to a most violent revolt by the governed against the government, poor against rich, workers against masters, wages against capital, proletariat against bourgeoisie: in a word, to a real civil war, or rather a social war; and if you take into account the unbridled licence of the press, the clubs and the posters, there was certainly no lack of fire-brands to spark off the conflagration.

Charles de Rémusat, *Mémoires*.

12 Radical Republicans: legalism and realism

As for the people, it has terrible grievances because of its suffering and despair. There are a mass of resentments, for the most part justified.

As for the government, our principle is at stake, the great principle of the Republic. Whatever errors may have been committed, there has been no violation of the sovereign right such as might justify a slide into the most terrible sort of war, a civil war.

... Instinctively, many said the Revolution should be political and social, and they were right! They were right from the point of view of speculative philosophy, even from the point of view of the logical and political consequences that might follow in a given period of time.

They were wrong when, disregarding the time factor, they wished to bring about the unknown immediately, to bring into practice what was but dimly comprehended, and to bring into reality an ideal that had been defined only vaguely.

From *La Réforme*, 24 June 1848.

13 Disillusioned Republicans

What is the sense, what is the point of the detestable battle which has, since yesterday, turned the streets of Paris into a bloodbath? What use is armed subversion?

With universal suffrage, freedom of the press and the right of association, all insurrection is absurd: it is an outrage against the sovereignty of the people and a crime against society. It is not permissible for a small minority to express its grievances, if it has any, by shooting people. . . . What good can this battle do? Who could change conditions for the proletariat in a single day?

Deceived by false appearances, led astray by promises that will not be kept, how many good men have perhaps already paid for their cruel mistakes with their lives? How many are there among the dead whose entire lives were devoted to the defence of those very workers who strike them down today? Yes, in this appalling, infinitely regrettable battle that has been joined, Republicans are falling on both sides.

We weep for them, and lament their passing. But we can only hate and despise those who work for disorder, who inspire the conflict and who conspire and pay for sedition with foreign gold. Order will be restored, for a society cannot abandon itself to the whim of a minority. It is both the duty and the right of society to continue to exist.

From *Le National*, 29 June 1848.

For my part, I have all my life long dreamt about a fraternal Republic based on the Gospels; that is to say, the triumph of reason, morality and justice. I have longed only for the coming of a form of government devoted to ensuring everybody's happiness, everybody's liberty and everybody's prosperity. So I am ashamed of my country and for modern civilization when I hear about the bloody orgies in which these so-called Republicans who are really enemies of the Republic have just been wallowing with such ferocity and ardour.

Our modern socialists, Louis Blanc, Proudhon, Pierre Leroux, Cabet, Raspail and others of that ilk – what sort of inspiration did they have, what sort of ideals, when they spread the poisoned venom of their fatal doctrines?

Are not the greatest enemies of liberty, those men who – by their very excess of zeal, by their dangerous speeches and their calls to class hatred – divide society, create enmity, call for revenge, appeal to brute force and oblige a nation to throw itself into the arms of a dictator or despot in order to escape from carnage, looting, devastation – in a word, from civil war?

Now that universal suffrage has been won, now that we have the freedom of the press and of opinion, the right of petition and discussion, it is criminal in the highest degree, before God and humanity, to bring about the triumph of one's ideas by brute force.

For my own part, this dreadful blood-letting in the streets of Paris has been the conflict between order and disorder, between liberty and anarchy, between good and evil, and between pure democracy and shameless terrorism and demagogy. In these events I can see the influence of Barbès and others, the venomous dreams of the socialists, the ambitions of all sorts of men who want power, and finally foreign gold, particularly from England.

M. Vachez, a leading moderate Republican at Lyon, in a
letter to Joseph Bergier of 29 June 1848 (contained in
J. Bergier, *Journal d'un bourgeois de Lyon en 1848*).

4 *In defence of civilization*

The struggle these last few days . . . has been clearly and forcefully delineated. Yes, on one side there stood order, liberty, civilization, the decent Republic, France; and on the other, barbarians, desperados emerging from their lairs for massacre and looting, and odious partisans of those wild doctrines that the family is only a word and property naught but theft.

From *Le National*, 29 June 1848.

Part Three
June 1848–May 1849

This was a period of increasing Conservative repression, during which in most areas the dominance of the Notables was reasserted. This, and the whole pattern of events after February, caused a polarization of political forces, driving most moderate Republicans either into alliance with other Conservatives in defence of social order, or else to the Left, in alliance with radicals and in defence of Republican institutions. The most notable political events were the election of Louis-Napoléon Bonaparte as president of the Republic with both Conservative and massive popular support, and the general elections of May 1849, which clearly revealed the political divisions existing in France and served as the next stage in the intensification of fear and bitterness.

1 Political alignments and re-alignments

The moderate Republicans make common cause with the constitutionalists and the Legitimists against the socialists whenever society is under violent attack. Then they make an about turn as soon as they see that the Republic in its turn is being threatened (or rather that control of the Republic is passing into the hand of others). We shall see the supporters of the monarchy resolutely making a show of Republicanism in order to fight socialism. Then, once that danger has passed, we shall see them return to their former convictions and to their old love.

Odilon Barrot, *Mémoires posthumes*.

2 Political polarization

The decent moderate Republican party has virtually disappeared from the assembly. We are situated between a small minority that wants a social or red republic and an immense majority that won't hear of a republic at any price.

Alexis de Tocqueville, in a letter to Gustave de Beaumont, 24 September 1848.

The exiles of June 1848, 'Go and teach' (Gospel of St Matthew). Following the repression of the June insurrection prisoners were deported to Algeria and other colonies.

3 Political repression

Article 1   Citizens have the right to meetings, under the following arrangements:

. . .

Article 2   The opening of any club or citizens' meeting shall be preceded by a declaration furnished by the founders (in Paris to the prefecture of police, in the departments to the mayor of the commune and to the prefect). . . .

. . .

Article 4   The authority in receipt of this declaration may in every instance designate a judicial or administrative official who shall attend the meetings of the club. . . .

. . .

Article 6   The members of the club shall not allow the discussion of any proposition contrary to public order or public morality.

Article 7   Reports, addresses and all other communications between clubs are forbidden. So too are all forms of affiliation between clubs. . . .

Article 13   Secret societies are forbidden.

From *Bulletin des lois de la République française*.

4 *Political isolation of the constituent assembly*

Following the June insurrection: There is no doubt about it. From then on many of us permitted ourselves to adopt more openly an attitude of sceptical mistrust toward ideas that were Republican (or simply even liberal) and to return in a more or less whimsical way to prejudices and methods that had been considered out-moded or doomed. With the sole exception of the principle of Legitimism, the difference between Legitimists and thorough-going Conservatives became weaker and weaker. A taste for tradition became fashionable: it was a sort of protest against the ambitions of democracy. This retrograde movement was not, however, very strong in the assembly, which never forgot its origins. That was, indeed, the factor which was gradually to alienate it from the country.

Charles de Rémusat, *Mémoires*.

5 *The need for moral order*

There is no hiding the fact: we live in a period when moral sense is totally expunged from the minds of the people in the big cities. That spirit of resignation which made the poor accept their station as something ordained by God, that sense of hierarchy which religion alone can inspire, has weakened as Christianity has lost its hold on the masses. The worker cannot see why he should lack everything when the rich man goes short of nothing. He revolts against this unjust distribution of wealth which, in his eyes, has ceased to be compensated for in any way. He blames our social system and sees some sort of justice in overthrowing it. He wants, in his turn, to enjoy all the good things of life. This becomes a consuming and intoxicating passion. It is no longer a question of a victory over some verbal quibble, or over the form of the government. What is at the root of these impious endeavours is the total reshaping of society. From political riots we have passed to social war.

    To so grave a malady there would be but one remedy – a return to moral and religious beliefs.

From *La Liberté*, published in Rouen, 3 July 1848.

6 The god of property

What is *the* problem today? It is the problem of creating respect for property in people who do not own any. Well, I know only one means of inspiring this respect, of making those who are not property owners believe in property. You have to make them believe in God – not some vague God defined by eclecticism or some such system, but the God of the catechism, the God who dictated the ten commandments and who gives robbers their everlasting punishment. That is the only genuinely popular belief that can protect property properly.

Property – it will be safe only if this simple faith is taught, the simple all-embracing, popular faith that was the foundation of our society for so many centuries.

From a speech by Montalembert to the national assembly,
20 September 1848 (in *Compte rendu des séances de
l'Assemblée nationale*, vol. IV).

7 Conservative fears unallayed

There was no time when Bordeaux did not see order maintained in its midst. But we must not hide the fact that dire passions there do not lack organs of expression. Some clubs that survived the general elections, and whose meetings were not public, kept the people in a certain state of excitement. The many supporters of good order became worried about this. It was known that anarchistic and terrorist doctrines were being urged there and that the insurgents of Paris, had they succeeded, would have found among the members of these clubs keen supporters ready to obey their orders, whatever they might be.

The vast majority of the population, workers included, is solidly for the maintenance of order.

From a report by the Procureur-général at Bordeaux,
22 July 1848 (Archives nationales BB[18] 1465).

8 Rumour or reality?

There is talk about the discovery of conspirators who are supposed to have plotted first to take over the gas works, to deprive the city of Lyon of gas light, then to beat the 'stand to' in the various districts of the city and kill the national guardsmen as they set out singly to report to their stations. After that, the plan was to seize control of the most important places and set fire to some districts inhabited chiefly by the rich. But somebody blew the gaff, and that led to investigations which resulted in the discovery of caches of torches that the incendiaries would have used, brand new guillotines that were to have been permanently set up, and a mass of other instruments of destruction.

M. Brossette, moderate Republican at Lyon, in a letter to
Joseph Bergier, 5 July 1848 (in J. Bergier, *Journal d'un
bourgeois de Lyon en 1848*).

9 *The threat remains*

Nobody has given up his claims. In the breasts of the masses the same ideas, hopes and passions are still simmering. Each feels around him something that says: 'What we have got isn't peace, it's just a truce; it isn't conciliation, it's just suppression. We bow our heads today, but we'll raise them again tomorrow.'

The deep-seated, fundamental trouble is the inexorable hate that now exists between the workers and the manufacturers, and between the proletariat and the bourgeoisie.

From a report by the councillor-delegate to the
commission of inquiry on the insurrection, Lyon,
30 July 1848.

10 *Need for strong government*

France needs moral order and material order, and any force determined to provide her with both is entitled to the sympathy and collaboration of right-thinking men.

A second struggle is a possibility, even a probability. It is because we believe it is probable that we consider it a duty to give energetic backing to the military triumvirate that is governing us at present.

It is for Conservatives like ourselves to back a government that supports our ideas.

We would be denying our past and our principles if we undermined a government that is working for order and trying to give back to the authorities the strength they have lost since the last revolution.

From *Mémorial Bordelais*, 18 July 1848.

11 *Official recognition of the danger*

It is gathered from information available to the government that the agitators, feeling powerless openly to attack the Republic by force, are endeavouring to wage ceaseless underground warfare against it. Secret societies are being formed again, both in Paris and in the provinces, into which emissaries are being sent to stir up more trouble.

From a circular from the minister of justice to the
Procureurs-généraux, 29 July 1848 (Archives nationales
BB^{18} 1472).

2 The Socialists reorganize

The above report doubtless exaggerates, although to what extent it is difficult to judge. However, such reports contributed to a heightening fear in government and conservative circles. Compare the report that follows with the preceding circular. Is it an accurate assessment of the situation, or does it tell the minister what he expected to hear?

I have drawn attention to the secret societies that are being formed on a vast scale, constituting a formidable block in the city of Lyon and the neighbouring communes. These societies recruit members principally from the communist groups of which there are many. . . . These groups draw membership primarily from the silk workers and the miners of the Loire coal-field.

From a report of the Procureur-général at Lyon,
2 August 1848 (ibid.).

RADICAL ORGANIZATION AND AIMS
The Solidarité Républicaine has been formed with the object of uniting in one band all the separate elements of democratic opinion, of directing them toward a common goal, and of setting on a firm footing the great party that works for a Democratic and Social Republic.

In the view of the founders of the Solidarité Républicaine, the Republic has never been anything less than the sole, true means of bringing about the reform of contemporary institutions insofar as these at present constitute an outrage to human dignity and a threat to the livelihood of the largest class in our society. The founders demand the right to work, just as they support the rights of property.

Part of a letter addressed by Solidarité Républicaine in
Paris to sympathizers in Lyon, 25 September 1848 (ibid.).

Article 19 The means of action available to the general council shall be the creation or support of democratic newspapers, the provision of information for voters, the guaranteeing of uncorrupt elections, and the distribution of all publications designed to inform and edify the population of towns and villages. It will help the workers to join together and assist with the formation of associations for the protection of all their members. It will come to the aid of all its members who are in difficulties because of unemployment or illness and will seek means of finding work for them. Finally, it will neglect no means or opportunity of ensuring that Republican ideas are respected and practised.

'Association pour le développement des droits et des intérêts de la démocratie': Solidarité Républicaine, rules, dated 4 November 1848 (in A. Lucas, *Les Clubs et les clubistes*).

13 *Continuing social unrest*

RESISTANCE TO THE FORTY-FIVE-CENTIME TAX

The newspapers opposed to the old executive commission have been fighting desperately and ceaselessly for two months against the imposition of this tax. Since the events of June they have redoubled their attacks. Our farmers really are incapable of paying and these press attacks, though confined within the limits of strict legality, have whipped up animosity among the peasants.

Report from the prefect of the Dordogne, 29 June 1848; presented as evidence to the commission of inquiry on the insurrection.

Resistance is being organized on a large scale. More than one hundred communes in the departments of Gers, Hautes-Pyrénées and Basses-Pyrénées are at present banding together. Emissaries are going round all the time recruiting supporters, and it seems they do not find recruiting difficult. Besides, those who are not willing to join are threatened with death or with having their homes set fire to. . . . We need infantry and artillery. . . . They talk of marching on Paris. This is hardly a serious threat. But it shows at least how keyed-up people are.

Report of the lieutenant of *gendarmerie* at Mirande, to the captain commanding at Auch, 11 June 1848 (Archives nationales BB[18] 1462–64).

At Laloubère (Haute-Pyrénées): Considerable numbers of the inhabitants armed themselves with axes, muskets and other weapons, and the alarm was raised by ringing a peal on the church bells. The clerks in the tax-office only just escaped a rough handling from the crowd.

Report of the Procureur-général at Pau, 30 August 1848 (ibid.).

HOSTILITY TO INDIRECT TAXES

On the 6th [of September], in the evening, a demonstration took place at Draguignan over the indirect taxes. Twenty-eight or thirty citizens, all members of the Democratic club, met together and, after some heavy drinking, went through the city singing the *Marseillaise*. They shouted slogans: 'Down with the gendarmerie' and 'Down with the consolidated tax.' But by 11 p.m. all was quiet again.

Report of the five-day period 11–15 September 1848 by the general officer commanding the 7th military division (Archives historiques du Ministère de la Guerre F^1 16).

FOREST DISORDERS

The sub-prefect of Saint-Gaudens wanted to restart forestry work in the woods at Arbas (Haute-Garonne). But a score-and-a-half men, all armed and in the sort of disguises that used to be worn by gangs called *demoiselles*,[1] drove off the workers who had been set to work. Several shots were fired.

Report on the five-day period 10–15 April 1849 by the general officer commanding the 10th military division (ibid.).

SOCIALIZING AND POLITICKING

On 6 March, eighty persons rushed through several streets in the town of Beaucaire chanting and shouting 'Raspail for ever! Barbès for ever!' It is also said that they shouted 'Three cheers for the guillotine'. Afterward, these persons, who are members of the Société de la Montagne, went back to their club. The rest of the night passed without incident.

Report on the five-day period 5–10 May 1849 by the general officer commanding the 8th military division (ibid.).

[1] i.e. in female clothing. *See* R. D. Price 'Popular Disturbances in the French Provinces after the July Revolution of 1830', *European Studies Review*, 1971.

A red flag was borne along the road from Dôle to Parcey (Jura) by M. Magdelaine of the commune of Ranans. Carrying this banner aloft, he shouted 'Raspail for ever! Barbès for ever! Up the Reds! Down with the Whites!' These seditious utterances gave rise to much excitement among the inhabitants of the commune of Villette. They thought a new revolution had broken out. . . .

The arrival at Morteau of M. Montalembert, a representative of the people, caused great excitement among the democrats. They all gathered under the windows of the mayor's house, where this representative had put up for the night, and planned to greet him with a *charivari*.[1]

Report on the five-day period 25–31 August 1849 by the
general officer commanding the 5th military division
(ibid.).

TRADITIONAL HOSTILITY, AND THE MEANS TO EXPRESS IT

In the commune of Cogny, *arrondissement* of Villefranche (Rhône), a placard has been nailed to the tree of liberty. It is couched in the following terms: 'Tremble, ye aristocrats of Cogny. Raspail is one of those elected. If certain blasphemers – those who did not vote for him – merit punishment, woe unto you, ye rich men of Cogny. Wicked rich men, blind men, open your eyes and you will recognize in this man Raspail the power of a God.'

Report on the five-day period 26–30 September 1848 by
the general officer commanding the 6th military division
(ibid.).

14 Radical Republicanism moves Leftward

The political problem is no longer just the problem of the future. A new problem has come to the fore, and democracy has had to emblazon its banner with the words: 'The democratic and social Republic.'

From *La Réforme*, 21 August 1848.

AGAINST A REPUBLIC OF FINANCIERS

The bankers and Jews have already gained over the Republic that disastrous influence they exerted over the monarchy.

From *La Réforme*, 8 August 1848.

[1] A traditional, noisy, cacophonous, and usually hostile reception indicative of elements of folklore being adapted to political situations.

5 The Conservative Republic

What we – the moderates, the immense majority of Frenchmen – need is the Republic *and* order. That is to say, no more clubs that stir up and deprave the people day after day. . . . . The Republic with a system of taxes that will not ruin the rich or well-to-do citizens – a ruin detrimental to the poor because making it impossible for the rich to employ them – and that will not cause the disappearance from our country, together with all wealth, of our luxury industries which are the staple of our export trade.

From *Le Constitutionnel*, 5 December 1848.

Against proposals in favour of progressive taxation : . . . It is not equal rights; that is just and moral. It is equality between ability and inability . . . between vice and virtue, that sort of equality which demands similar advantages for dissimilar rights, that equality which leads to barbarism and destruction of morality. . . .
    (Hear, hear!)

From a speech by M. Lherbette in the debate on a new constitution, 25 September 1848 (in *Compte rendu des séances de l'Assemblée nationale*, vol. IV).

6 Debate on the constitution: powers of the president of the Republic

. . . Centralization . . . meant that the whole administration of the country, from the greatest to the most trivial matters, would be in the President's hands; all the thousands of officials controlling the whole land could depend upon no one but him. . . . In such conditions who could be the president elected by the people unless he were a pretender to the throne? The institution could serve the turn only of somebody wishing to transform presidential into royal power.

Alexis de Tocqueville, *Recollections*.

7 Conservative contempt for parliamentarians

At the National Assembly half the session was wasted debating the current pronunciation of the word *club*. Some said *cleubbe*, others *clu* to rhyme with *plu*. It was decided to adopt the pronunciation *club*.

Maréchal de Castellane, *Journal*, entry under 25 July 1848.

18 The presidential elections

Marx wrote in his preface to The Eighteenth Brumaire *that his purpose was to 'demonstrate how the class struggle in France created circumstances and relationships that made it possible for a grotesque mediocrity to play a hero's part'. It seems exaggerated to describe in these terms a man who, possessing little more than the glamour of his family name, was able to take advantage of the political situation, seize power and maintain it for twenty years.*

Electors!

Our poverty is growing worse every day! Why?

Because those who govern us inspire no confidence; that is the point.

What have they done to deserve our confidence?

The unfortunate die of hunger.

The worker has no employment.

The peasant has no market for his crops.

The shop-keeper can sell nothing.

The landowner no longer receives his rents.

The capitalist no longer dares to put out his funds for lack of security.

France, which used to be so rich: in what sort of a state is it now?

National bankruptcy is to be feared, and it is a threat to each and every one of us.

For CONFIDENCE, the source of a nation's prosperity, to be re-established we need at the head of the government a man who has the backing of the country.

Napoléon saved France from anarchy at the time of the first revolution.

The great man's nephew with his magical name will give us security and will save us from impoverishment.

Enclosed with a report by the Procureur-général at Metz,
1 December 1848 (Archives nationales BB[18] 1471).

THE DEVELOPMENT OF BONAPARTIST SENTIMENTS
Nowhere does the forty-five-centime surtax encounter more resistance than in this department. Republican opinion in the Ruffec *arrondissement* seems to have met with a perceptible set-back, and the land-workers, as if drawn along in the wake of their neighbours in the department of Charente-Inférieure, now set all their hopes on Louis-Napoléon.

Report of the Procureur-général at Bordeaux, 18 July
1848; presented as evidence to the commission of inquiry
on the insurrection.

Louis-Napoléon's candidature is going forward by leaps and bounds. . . .
The French want dragoon government and they'll get it. Our hillsides and
valleys re-echo on all sides to the cry 'Napoléon forever!' It is turning
people's heads: it is mass hysteria. Napoléon is regarded as heaven-sent.
He's the man, they say, who will save France. I am just back from Lyon
which was all for Cavaignac a week ago. Well, today I saw people ripping
up his election posters everywhere. His handbills are being torn up and are
littering the streets. All you can hear are shouts of 'Louis-Napoléon for
ever!' and 'Down with Cavaignac.'

M. Pagany, in a letter to Joseph Bergier, 8 December 1848
(in J. Bergier, *Journal d'un bourgeois de Lyon en 1848*).

WORKERS FOR BONAPARTE

The Emperor's nephew appeared as the workers' friend and was expected
to bring back the days of work and plenty. . . . The other candidates could
only, in our view, perpetuate the terrible period of poverty in which we
lived.

We had no intention of causing harm. Order is essential if we are to have
work to do.

An appeal for pardon by three workers at Grandvilliers
(Oise), forwarded by the Procureur-général at Amiens
along with his report of 26 August 1849. The workers had
been found guilty of causing a disturbance out of their
over-enthusiasm for Louis-Napoléon during the
elections (Archives nationales BB^{24} 361–68).

THE BANDWAGON EFFECT

I must admit that I consider the election of Bonaparte highly likely. And
what makes that eventuality more likely is precisely the fact that it seems
likely. It is easy to see that many are looking toward the horizon where that
particular sun may rise. Even among those who support Cavaignac's
candidature there are plainly many who take pains not to get on the wrong
side of the other party. The language – or rather, the silence – of the newspapers should make this quite clear to you.

Alexis de Tocqueville, in a letter to Gustave de Beaumont,
12 October 1848.

Were not Prince Louis borne forward on a surge of popular opinion which
overwhelms us, I would understand how the meeting might put up a
candidate. But this is not the position we are in. We cannot withstand the

Satire on the political behaviour of the 'most spirited' of peoples, as the current of opinion in favour of Louis-Napoléon grew.

enthusiasm of a popular movement which is proof against all rational argument. Our situation is such that we ought not to put forward a candidate.

Adolphe Thiers, speaking at the meeting of Conservative
politicians known as the *réunion de la rue de Poitiers*;
reported in *La Gazette de France*, 5 November 1848.

History affords no parallel to this spectacle of all the eminent men of all the former political parties uniting in support of a man whom no one of them would personally have selected. They in fact follow, while they assume to direct, a popular impulse which they could not resist. The memory of the Emperor Napoléon is no doubt a master spell in this impulse; but the hatred of the Republic gives another signification to the name of Bonaparte, and the traditional recollection that it was by this means that the last Republic in France was destroyed gives double force to this mode of protestation.

Lord Normanby, *Journal of a Year of Revolution*.

9 The appeal of the Conservative Bonaparte

An immense mass of honest workers and industrious farm labourers, who want to see the end of policies of disorder and brigandage – all those who detest the red Republic, bankruptcy and the guillotine – the conscientious and enlightened men of no matter what persuasion – the supporters of religion, property and the family – France, in a word, the real France with its admirable instincts for order, and its hatred of demagogy – that is what Louis-Napoléon Bonaparte's party is made up of.

Originally published in *L'Indépendant de l'Ouest*,
reproduced in *La Gazette de France*, 13 December 1848.

0 General Cavaignac's candidature

General Cavaignac has been losing more ground, and the cabinet has satisfied no one, just like the executive commission. The anarchists find it is too concerned about preserving law and order, and the supporters of law and order consider it is too well disposed toward the anarchists.

Alexis de Tocqueville, in a letter to Gustave de Beaumont,
12 October 1848.

21 Anti-Bonapartist propaganda

It is enough to analyse the elements of the party, or rather of the various parties, whose candidate is M. Louis Bonaparte, in order to be able to appreciate the immense dangers that would be created by the success of such a candidate, if, by some impossible chance, our universal suffrage was dazzled for an instant by the Napoleonic razzmatazz. There is a bit of everything in this queer hotch-potch of contradictory emotions which all tend at least to one common object, the destruction of the Republic through the triumph of our native prejudices.

You find them, all mixed up – Bonapartism, communism, royalism, reaction – all linked by a common animosity toward the Republic, either because of what it has given, or what it has not given, and will never give to the old Conservatives, to the members of the old Left, the old Left-centre, to the Monarchists supporting all varieties of opinion and all the various dynasties, to the partisans of the most anti-social ideas. . . . They conceal beneath the candidature their regrets, hopes, mutually hostile plans. Linking together for this battle they only wait for the moment of victory to break up into splinter groups. M. Louis Bonaparte has given hostages to every system and to every party. Now he girds himself with the overalls of socialism to go along with one section of the workers, now he dons the little Napoléonic hat to appease the Imperialists. He makes himself out to be a Conservative to please M. Thiers or M. Molé. Which of these policies would he be able to follow?

From *Le National*, 1 December 1848.

[It is not true that] the imperial name is a guarantee of order and security. Order by means of despotism is a possibility. But it is not that sort of order which the French Republic desires. Security? But how? By means of war, perhaps. For if his name evokes any memories, they are certainly memories of war. Those wars were glorious wars, it is true. But then, so far, it is not exactly by embarking on foreign wars that people have sought to ensure security at home.

From *Le National*, 6 December 1848.

Cavaignac . . . has neither the prestige of a name nor the power of the head of a dynasty. He would be a president for only a short term and with very limited powers. Consequently, the day he wants to drag France into adventures he will smash himself against the national will. We shall not get away so easily with the other who, whether we desire it or not, will, in the popular opinion, be a king from the start and will later become king in reality. That is where the logic of events leads us. At a parade, some regiments will shout 'Napoléon for ever!' The faubourgs will follow suit and that will be the end of it. It will be like Spanish America, subject to the whim of the mob and of the soldiery. What a happy and glorious prospect!

Jules Martinelli, *Un mot sur le situation*, a pamphlet published at Bordeaux during the campaign.

22 *The people go to the polls*

In the depths of the country, the imperial procession will make its way toward this or that canton. At its head come a few old men, veterans rejuvenated by a glint of history and convinced they are marching as they did forty years back, under the soaring eagle.

The column is flanked by the priest and the local gentry with Napoléon on their lips and Henri V in their hearts. Next come the decent, honest workers who worship a name because they have never understood what it signified and who follow an anachronism as if it were a guiding star. They are desperate because of the poverty that threatens to engulf them.

From *La Réforme*, 11 December 1848.

23 Louis-Napoléon Bonaparte: Prince President of the Republic

He was a great deal better than the impression one might fairly have formed of him from his earlier career and mad enterprises. That was my first impression as I got to know him. In this he disappointed his adversaries, but perhaps he disappointed his friends even more, if one can give that name to the politicians who supported his candidature. For most of them had chosen him, not for his worth, but for his presumed mediocrity. They thought he would be a tool for them to use at will and break any time they wanted. In this they were mightily deceived.

Alexis de Tocqueville, *Recollections*.

24 Conservative unity in defence of their Republic

It is important to recall that we are not now enjoying one of those periods of constitutional calmness. We have just come through a revolutionary cataclysm; the ground has hardly had time to become firm again. Everything is still shaking. It will not do to see on one side a government party and on the other an opposition with nothing very much between them except a few details of emphasis. What is at stake is not a political system: it is the very existence of society. The executive does not merely represent the triumph of a party. Its task is to support and defend the fate of all civilization. Whosoever, in order to show himself independent of the executive today, wished to add to our liberties, could only give us excesses or abuses. The government, that is to say, society, is confronted by socialism.

That means the executive has an immense task, and all those who desire society's continued existence have no right, as far as the present is concerned, to haggle over giving it support. People really must consider what is happening. The old parties, so deeply separated under the monarchy by their principles about the origins and rights of the executive, are one today in giving immediate support to the great task of saving society. All the demagogues vilify this coalition which constitutes the unconquerable strength we oppose to them. They present it as a pact against the Republic. The demagogues say that, but they do not believe it. They know full well that to consolidate this union we cannot rekindle the very passions that used to divide us; and they know that, if we did not cleave together, we would foster anarchy and socialism by our disagreements.

From *Le Constitutionnel*, 19 February 1849.

25 The old parties survive

On the 11th of this month a Legitimist banquet attended by some 200 persons took place at Lunel. After it shouts of 'Long live Henri V' and 'Down with the Republic' were heard.

Report on the five-day period 10–15 March 1849 by the general officer commanding the 8th military division (Archives historiques du Ministère de la Guerre F¹ 16).

26 Elections to the legislative assembly

PROGRAMME OF THE COMITÉ DÉMOCRATE-SOCIALISTE OF THE SEINE

1 The Republic stands superior to the rights of majorities.
2 If the Constitution is violated, the representatives of the people should give the lead in resisting.
3 There must be loyalty between nations, such as there is between men. The use of the power of France against the freedom of peoples is a crime and a *violation of the constitution*. France owes aid to nations fighting tyranny.
4 The right to work is the first of all rights. It is the right to live – the most intolerable of tyrannies is the tyranny of capitalism. The representatives of the nation can, and should, set out to abolish this tyranny.
5 In a free nation, education should be universal, free, the same for all, egalitarian and obligatory.
6 Calling in the milliard francs[1] belonging to those who had fled from France because of the Revolution is a just, useful and feasible measure.

Published in *La Réforme*, 20 April 1849.

A RADICAL REPUBLICAN ELECTORAL MEETING

On the evening of 8 May there took place at Bédarieux (Hérault) a public meeting attended by some fifteen to eighteen hundred people. It was chaired by M. Bonnal, a goldsmith. M. Sabatier and M. Azémar, the socialist candidates, were present. Very violent speeches were made, and the rights of property and the family were attacked. It was said the elections of 10 December were just a surprise, and, believing they were electing Napoléon the Great, the people had in fact merely voted for Napoléon the cossack, the play-boy, the addle-pate, and so on. . . . Finally, they proclaimed that the Red Flag surmounted by a phrygian cap was the sole emblem capable of representing the liberation of the people and the glorious memory of '93.

[1] Compensation paid after the Restoration in 1815 to *emigrés* whose land had been confiscated during the Revolution.

The meeting concluded with three great bursts of applause for Ledru-Rollin, the great liberator of the people.

Report on the five-day period 5–10 May 1849 by the
general officer commanding the 8th military division (in
Archives historiques du Ministère de la Guerre F^1 16).

CONSERVATIVE ELECTION PROPAGANDA
In the form of a dialogue between two brothers:
PIERRE: Society is badly organized, the professors say. My friend, there are mountains of pride and ignorance in this assertion, for it is God who has the biggest part in the organization of society by means of the laws He imposes on nature, through instincts, emotions and all the needs He has given man, as well as the different ways of satisfying them. Human beings only need to make laws to prevent bad men from disturbing the good.

Work – that is the source of everything. It is the best way of sharing things. Each receives in due measure according to the strength, effort and intelligence that God has given him. That is why equality is a deceptive notion. . . . If God had desired that, He could have made all men in the same mould. Instead of that, He made them very unequal in every particular. Can I be the equal of your neighbour, Nicholas, who, instead of working like me from dawn to nightfall, spends half his time in the pub? Have I got to share my grain and my cabbages with him? . . . There will always be poor and rich, strong men and weak men, clever men and stupid men, or men with little wit, spendthrifts and savers. The first, the greatest of all the ways of improving the people's lot is to bring back morality and to bring back good sense. For a century efforts have been made to destroy people's religious beliefs and their respect for authority as represented by the law, family ties and love and regard for parents. In a word, people have been taught to despise all that is decent and sacred. At the same time as all this was being destroyed, people were being taught about rights that are for the most part absurd or dangerous. . . . The people have been given desires and passions that no government could ever satisfy. . . .

The poverty reported in the towns, especially the big ones, is principally the result of the irregular, immoral lives of the workers.

Maréchal Bugeaud, duc d'Isly, *Veillées d'une chaumière de la
Vendée*, an election pamphlet published at Lyon.

ELECTION RESULTS: CONSERVATIVE REACTIONS
The Conservatives, who for six months had seen all the by-elections going in their favour, and who filled and dominated almost all the local councils, had come to put unlimited confidence in the system of universal franchise,

which had formerly filled them with unlimited mistrust. So, in the election that had just taken place, they had expected not only to defeat, but to annihilate their adversaries, and they were as downcast at falling short of the triumph of which they had dreamed as they would have been if they really had been defeated.

. . . One hundred and fifty Montagnards had been elected. Some of the peasants and most[1] of the soldiers had voted for them; it was the two main anchors of mercy that threatened to snap in the storm. The terror was universal: it retaught the various monarchical parties the virtues of tolerance and modesty, virtues which they had cultivated after February, but which had been largely forgotten during the last six months. On all sides it was recognized that there was no longer a possibility of changing from a Republic for the present, and that all there remained to be done was to get the moderate Republicans to oppose the Mountain.

Alexis de Tocqueville, *Recollections*.

27 *Growing appeal of a Bonapartist solution*

It seems that the election will not be as good as was expected. Socialism has made the most alarming strides; in several of the departments the Red candidates will be successful, and even if the moderates succeed in others, their majority will be so small that the moral effect will be disastrous. If this happens there will be nothing left to do but to pack our things, get up a civil war and ask the cossacks to come and help us!

. . . The Empire is the only thing that can save the situation. Some of the leading politicians have been nibbling at the idea. . . .

Letter from M. Morny to Mme de Flahault, 16 May 1849;
in Earl of Kerry (ed.), *The Secret of the Coup d'État*.

28 *Conservatives move Right*

[In the Assembly] the Legitimist party was well represented. It commanded perhaps 140 votes. That was a lot – too many, even, with regard to its numerical strength and its popularity in the country. But its support was essential in the elections, as was also that of the clergy. Not the least striking proof of the general need to resist the onslaught of the Revolutionary parties at any price was the ease with which bourgeois France, forgetting its prejudices and resentments, had agreed to give more support to the Right than it was entitled to expect to have in normal circumstances.

Charles de Rémusat, *Mémoires*.

[1] A false impression.

Part Four
May 1849–December 1851

This was a period of continual crisis. Economic difficulties maintained mass discontent and helped make possible in many areas the continued organization of démocrate-socialiste support. This fact kept buoyant Conservative fears of social revolution. Whatever the divisions among conservative Notables, an alliance of Conservatives survived. But, unable as they were to agree on a solution to the problems of France, the members of this alliance were increasingly drawn toward accepting a Bonapartist – that is, an authoritarian – solution. Besides intensified police repression, the most notable acts of general repression during this period were the new education law, designed to increase the role of the Church in primary teaching, and legislation designed to restrict the electoral suffrage, by imposing stricter residence requirements.

1 Further political polarization: moderate Republicans move Leftward

DECLARATION BY THE ASSOCIATION DÉMOCRATIQUE DES AMIS DE LA CONSTITUTION

Today there are only two parties left in Europe – the party of Revolution, and the party of counter-Revolution; only two principles – democracy and despotism.

The days for middle-of-the-road policies and hesitation have passed.

Published in *Le National*, 22 May 1849.

How has it been possible for those middle classes whose emancipation began with the revolution of '89, who rejoiced at the abolition of the privileges of clergy and military, who would have been reduced again by the Restoration to the status they had under the Ancien Régime and on whose necks the July monarchy tried to load a new aristocracy – an aristocracy of money – how, we ask, how could these middle classes join forces with their former enemies against the people, their indispensable allies?

From *Le National*, 5 March 1850.

Senior officials at a ball given by the President of the Republic: 'A year ago we were made to dance to a different tune. . . . They can make their revolutions, we shall always come up top'.

2 *Radical Republican demonstration: 13 June 1849*

This impious war fought by the mother of Republics against the noble Roman Republic. . . . What it amounts to is the betrayal of the democratic cause; the Revolution has been given over into the power of kings. Cemented with our brave soldiers' blood, a sacrilegious alliance against the people has been formed with Austrians and cossacks, aristocrats and royalists.

In opposition to the government and to a parliamentary majority that formed a coalition against the constitution, law, justice, and the righteous cause of the liberty of the peoples, *insurrection was paramountly legitimate*. . . . This action was . . . a peaceful insurrection, constitutional and legally right.

Victor Considérant, *Journée du 13 juin 1849. Simples explications à mes amis et à mes commettants*, Paris 1849.

The Red newspapers were preaching armed revolution today. The workers have turned a deaf ear to the provocations of the Montagnard deputies. Furthermore, they have declared that, if they want them to take to the streets, they would have to march at their head. That is hardly to their taste.

I had had reliable information from the faubourg Saint-Jacques. The police commissioner, who is very intelligent, knew that after the terrible losses caused by the cholera . . . the workers would refuse to march. The movement would therefore only be the work of six or seven thousand extremists.

Maréchal de Castellane, *Journal*, entry under 12 June 1849.

Disorder in Lyon: government response

Quite a large number of persons has been arrested since 16 June, both in the city of Lyon and in the nearby communes. A fairly large quantity of arms has also been seized by columns of troops dispatched from Lyon into the suburbs and the neighbouring communes.

Report on the five-day period 16–20 June 1849 by the general officer commanding the 6th military division (Archives historiques du Ministère de la Guerre F^1 16).

Popular print portraying insurrection at Lyon in June 1849.

4 Atmosphere of unrest

On the night of 15/16 July part of the population of the faubourg of Nismes, in celebration of St Henry's Day[1] took part in noisy demonstrations and fired pistol shots. . . . On 27 July in the evening, to mark the anniversary of the July festivities,[2] their political opponents held a counter-demonstration.

Report on the five-day period 25–31 July 1849 by the
general officer commanding the 8th military division
(ibid.).

5 Radical demonstration of strength

The funeral of M. Laponneraye, chief editor of the newspaper *La Voix du peuple*, took place on 2 September at Marseilles. Four to five thousand people attended.

Report on the five-day period 31 August–1 September
1849 by the general officer commanding the 7th military
division (ibid.).

6 Accident or social protest?

Regarding the numerous outbreaks of fire : It must be noted that such outbreaks of fire are increasing in a remarkable fashion, causing great loss to rich and well-to-do-people.

Report on the five-day period 15–20 September 1849 by
the general officer commanding the 10th military
division (ibid. F[1] 17).

7 Cholera epidemic accentuates the social bitterness

A crowd of some three hundred made its way on 13 August at 9 p.m. to the town hall at Rochefort. The ringleaders said the poor people were being poisoned, that they alone were being attacked by the cholera and that the rich were safe against it.

Report on the five-day period 10–15 August 1849 by the
general officer commanding the 12th military division
(ibid.).

[1] In homage to the Legitimist pretender.

[2] In reply, a celebration of the July Revolution of 1830.

A Radical Republican celebration

The Ribeauvillé *gendarmerie* reports that M. Beisser, who was accused of political offences and cleared by the jury at Besançon, received an incredible ovation on his return home. There was a procession of youths and men with red handkerchiefs and ties, the road was lined with fir saplings draped with red, white and blue bunting, and triumphal arches with inscriptions were erected, one of them in front of his house. . . . Musket shots were fired, fireworks let off on the nearby mountainside, and the fire-brigade band performed. . . . [There were] many shouts of 'Up the Reds!'

Report on the five-day period 15–20 November 1849 by
the general officer commanding the 4th military division
(ibid. F[1] 16).

Preparing for revolt, or means of avoiding taxes?

The *gendarmerie* at Alais (Gard) discovered . . . a clandestine gunpowder factory. Utensils, bullet moulds and made-up cartridges were seized, as well as ammunition for pistols and muskets. Two persons . . . were apprehended.

Report on the five-day period 15–20 June 1849 by the
general officer commanding the 8th military division
(ibid.).

Conservative unity and moral re-education
for the masses

When all society, along with religion, morals, its dearest interests, its sacrosanct eternal laws, suddenly became the object of endless and ruthless attacks; when the most fundamental notions of truth, justice and right, without which no human society can continue to exist for a single day, had to be accounted for and defended; when unfathomable moral disorder was suddenly seen in our very midst – then all wise men, all true friends of our country, understood that it was no longer a question of knowing by whom and exactly how the good work would be done. It was a question of knowing that all the moral forces in the country had to be gathered together and that all must stand shoulder to shoulder to fight and conquer the common foe.

From a speech by M. Beugnot, reporter of the extra-
parliamentary committee examining proposals for a law
on education, in the assembly (*Compte rendu des
séances de l'Assemblée nationale législative*, vol. II).

11 Education Law (Loi Falloux) of 1849: Radical Republican reaction

To the countryfolk:
You must be told, in the first place, that old-style royalists are at the helm. Yes, my friends, your dear nephew of the Emperor, your choice of 10 December, who was supposed to make things so much better for you, has formed an alliance with the Whites, with those royalists who have twice let foreigners come right into the heart of our land.

All that brood which we threw out ignominiously in 1830 has once more appeared under the protection of M. Louis Bonaparte.

You never find a royalist without a Jesuit. The two make a pair. And Jesuits, missionaries and ignoramuses means wild sermons and the persecution of all that is educated, enlightened and intelligent; it means the domination of the family by the confessional, the abolition of science, and the suppression of all books except the catechism and the missal.

A population that can neither read nor write and has no other source of instruction but the parish priest's sermons does not understand public affairs at all. So it lets itself be led along like a troop of sheep by absolutely anybody, without being able to tell the difference between a shepherd and a butcher. They are fair game for royalists, usurers and tax-collectors.

From *La Voix de Peuple*, 22 December 1849.

12 Louis-Napoléon the nation's hope, above all parties

To strengthen the Republic, which is threatened by anarchy from so many directions, and, in foreign affairs, to maintain the name of France on a level commensurate with its reputation, men are needed who are inspired by an unshakeable love of their country and who will appreciate the need for unified and firm government and for clearly formulated policies, who will not compromise the central power by any irresolution, who are as well aware of my responsibility as of their own, who are men of action as well as of words. . . . The danger of riots in the streets was scarcely over when we saw the old parties begin to raise their banners again. . . . Amid this confusion France was worried because it did not see which direction it was going in. It looked to the control, to the leadership, and to the will of the man it elected on 10 December. Now, this will can only be felt if there is a community of ideas, opinions and convictions between the president and his ministers, and if the assembly associates itself with the thought of the nation as expressed in the election of the head of the executive. A whole system triumphed on 10 December, for the name Napoléon is in itself a programme. At home it means order, authority, religion and the welfare of the people; and abroad it means national self-respect. This policy, which began with my election, I shall, with the support of the national assembly and of the people, lead to its final triumph.

Message from Louis-Napoléon to the national assembly justifying his dismissal of the Barrot ministry, 31 October 1849 (in *Compte rendu des séances de l'Assemblée nationale législative*, vol. III).

3 Dismissal of the Barrot ministry: its significance

There are accidental and superficial causes which may have precipitated the present crisis. But the deep, permanent cause is, on the one hand, the conviction which the president had formed that not only would we not help him in the eventual *coup d'état*, but that we would not let him work toward it . . . [and], on the other hand, his desire himself to govern and, above all, to be seen himself to govern.

. . . There are several major sections of the [Conservative] majority that seem irretrievably alienated and determined not to help in the re-establishment of the Empire. I should not dare say the same about most of them. I even incline to the view that the president might easily win their support again and persuade them to serve his plans if he desired to do so and had the necessary ability. This majority that dislikes the Empire likes the Republic even less. Above all they are scared about letting the Reds in. Rather than them, they would throw themselves into the arms of the very devil.

Alexis de Tocqueville, in a letter to Gustave de Beaumont, 4 November 1849.

4 The weakness of Conservative resistance to Louis-Napoléon's ambitions

The Legitimists who had been used to independence for a long time constituted the parliamentary strength of the majority. This, with the exception of a select band that had not forsworn its principles, was made up of frightened Conservatives, Orléanists lacking any real sense of purpose, and former civil servants who were used to seeing the executive as the real government.

Charles de Rémusat, *Mémoires*.

5 Early 1850: Conservative view of the political situation

Our country could hardly be in a more critical position. Paris has improved a little, but the provinces are terrible. Socialism is making remarkable progress there. The government does not know which way to turn. The president of the Republic is at his wit's end, crippled by debts and surrounded by adventurers. He has a fixed idea that his destiny is under an imperial star, and so he is fatally attracted to every sort of wild idea. He has raised his banner before the national assembly. The assembly, riddled by petty passions and puerile notions, at the beck and call of old politicians with gangrene in their hearts, is making vain efforts to become a strong force in the land. The heterogeneous elements that constitute the majority there fights among itself for supremacy. The Legitimists . . . do not wish to make any concessions whatsoever, and remain what they always have been – over-ambitious, anachronistic and brainless. . . . The Orléanists have neither convictions nor affections: all they have are jealousies, prejudices and ambitions. Both parties reject every advance by the Republicans. . . . They will not hear of it, and their theme is 'The Republic is not possible!' Yet that is the only common ground on which all decent people could meet in order to save the nation. The Republicans are spurned, treated with insolence and peevishness, so they are turning to the Reds. Amid all this, the poltroons and the retired colonels, the old warrant officers and the peasants who were in the army are shouting 'Long live the Emperor!'

General Le Flô, a deputy in the national assembly, in a
letter to General Pelissier, 14 February 1850.

16 *Paris, March 1850: by-election results*

There is no hiding the fact: this nomination, by one hundred and twenty-six thousand votes, of a man who had been sentenced to transportation,[1] has created a deplorable impression . . . seen as a symptom of the strength that remains in ideas of revolt and insurrection. . . . The confidence that was growing each day has disappeared and been displaced by anxiety. . . . The fall in government stock points to another panic on the part of the capitalists.

From *Le Constitutionnel*, 16 March 1850.

17 *Growing anti-parliamentary feeling*

As far as we are concerned, it is quite plain that neither the parliamentarians nor the Legitimist party, nor the Orléanist party, nor the Revolutionary, have the solution that is needed – and needed at once. Not one of them is capable of solving the crisis and governing the country. All the new approaches, all the efforts made in any of these quarters, would lead only

[1] Deflotte, sentenced after the June Insurrection, beneficiary of a subsequent amnesty.

to delusions and disasters. Having once arrived at this conviction we needs must be led to examine and analyse the fifth source of power, stability and government still available to our society. We have to see whether the situation of the President of the Republic is not alone in offering this solution to the problem for which it would be vain to search elsewhere.

From *Le Constitutionnel*, 2 May 1850.

Republicans in defence of universal suffrage . . .

So long as universal suffrage is respected, so long as this great institution that represents the essence of the February Revolution remains intact, this ark of the covenant which is the very soul of the Republic, for so long we shall resign ourselves, under protest, even to the most unjust laws. . . . But when universal suffrage is tainted at its source, falsified in its action – then there will be naught in France save lies and oppression. Citizens worthy of the name will then have no other course open to them but to search through the constitution to see whether there is not some means of defending and saving liberty.

From *Le National*, 23 March 1850.

. . . Or not?

Following the new electoral law of May 1850, effectively restricting the suffrage: By standing aloof from those struggles in the streets which they were tempted to take part in because of scandalous provocations, by going no farther than declaring in petitions what attacks had been made on a principle guaranteed by the fundamental charter, the people has denied those who sought civil war, and wished to provoke riots, the sole weapon they had been intending to use in order to destroy at a blow all the liberties that we still have. . . . Every infringement of our rights, every attack on our principles and every attack on persons means new conquests for us, bringing us new recruits and swelling our ranks.

From *Le National*, 1 June 1850.

Radical Republican appeal to the army

It is indicative of a growing will to resist at least among some Republicans: Soldiers! See them for the hypocrites and infamous scoundrels that they are, those who would talk of discipline in order to make you march out and attack the rights of the people. For the people's rights are your rights. That sort of discipline is the discipline of mercenaries, those vile slaves of despotism who blindly obey the most barbarous orders. It is the discipline of cossacks. But the French soldier owes unquestioning obedience only in the face of the enemy. At home he is entitled to examine the orders he receives and to refuse to carry them out if they appear to him to be illegal and against the public interest. That is what Republican discipline is. . . . Everywhere in the regiments the Patriots who know one another and who can rely on one another must act together. They should form small groups of friends. The moment the great voice of the people is heard, the army must reply. With a unanimous shout going up all along the line, it must refuse to obey the bloody orders of officers who have sold their souls to the authorities.

Issued early in 1850 by the Comité Central de Résistance
(Archives of the Paris Prefecture of Police Aa. 432).

21 *Order depends on the army*[1]

When the very ground seemed to be trembling beneath our feet, the army was the sole monument that remained firm, the last rock that withstood the surge of revolution. This is because the army is above all else the stronghold of tradition and honour. In the midst of a society which hard times has made sceptical, selfish and eager for personal profit, the army has remained noble, inspired by principles of self-denial and devotion to duty, seeking its reward not in creature comforts, but in the honour and respect that attach to the designation *soldier*.

From *Le Constitutionnel*, 1 January 1850.

A MILITARY PRESENCE

There is still a lot of grumbling among the people. At Lyon there is much poverty. The ringleaders take advantage of it to stir up discontent. There is also less and less employment in Saint-Étienne. The socialist cafés are almost all packed out. The ringleaders proclaim that the end of the people's suffering is at hand. . . .

At Lyon, thanks to the declaration of a state of siege, the democrats, who have no arms, now seem to have made up their minds not to try anything so long as the garrison remains stationed there. The truth is that there is not, among the Lyon leaders of democracy, much sign of ardour. Above all, they do not have any excessive enthusiasm for starting a fight.

Maréchal de Castellane, *Journal*, entry under 9 April 1851.

[1] On the importance of the army acting in a police role in politics, *see* R. D. Price 'The French Army and the Revolution of 1830', *European Studies Review*, 1973.

The commanding officer cannot be everywhere; hence he cannot foresee everything in each particular case. The officer commanding on the spot will act with the utmost vigour. An officer who displays indecision will be held to blame and will have to answer for his conduct. Never should troops show indecision in the face of the mob. . . .

Troops will never permit the approach of a column of rioters or of women or children. Any hesitation on the part of infantry in opening fire may jeopardize it and lead to its being disarmed. At two hundred yards the rioters should be called upon to stop. If they do not obey, open fire immediately. The women and children operate by murdering the officers. They are the vanguard of the enemy. They must be treated as such.

'Confidential order' of 21 October 1850 from Maréchal de
Castellane, as general officer commanding the 5th and 6th
military divisions (in Maréchal de Castellane, *Journal*).

2 *Youthful high spirits, or political threat?*

Several young people rushed along one of the streets in the town, with a red, white and blue flag emblazoned with the words 'Society for the friends of Worthy Men'. Afterward they went into a café where they sang seditious songs. The slogan 'Up the Reds!' was shouted repeatedly.

Report, typical of those being sent at this time from all
over France, of the Procureur-général at Aix, 30 July 1850
(Archives nationales BB^{30} 358).

3 *Radical organizations consolidate*

In the departments of Haute-Saône, Doubs and Jura there is a clandestine society which is still not properly organized. It is trying to assimilate the old *Bons Cousins* brotherhood, which had many adherents in Franche-Comté and has appropriated its name. . . . The *Bons Cousins*, a half-masonic, half-political club, has existed in Franche-Comté from time immemorial. The demagogues made use of this set-up, either to conceal their doings more effectively or else in order to attract all the *Bons Cousins* in the neighbourhood.

Maréchal de Castellane, *Journal*, entry under 8 October
1850.

THE DIFFUSION OF IDEAS
In Saint-Étienne there are 722 cafés or pubs; that means 722 meetings every

evening. At them, ten or a dozen workers, while they have a drink, discuss political questions and pass the word from one to another.

Ibid., entry under 26 October 1850.

LYON: RADICAL PROPAGANDA
Prayer of the Voraces of the Croix-rousse: Our Father which art in the Tuileries, expunged be Thy name, Thy kingdom crumble. Thy will be ignored on this earth as it is in all others. Forgive us our victories as we forgive them to those whose names have become famous, and lead us not into collapsing under the weight of Thy vengeance, but deliver us of Thy presence.

Archives of the Paris Prefecture of Police Aa. 432.

I believe in God, the father of the people, maker of the Republic, in His only daughter the Goddess of the Republic, and in Jesus-Christ, the first republican who was the first to be sold by His generals.

Ibid.

24 *Problems of repression*

In spite of surveillance by the authorities, the agents of red democracy, the hawkers of brochures, pamphlets and newspapers are criss-crossing our Departments.

From *L'Ami du Peuple*, 9 May 1850.

*Dr Reaction's treatment
of the press.*

'Don't go too quickly':
Louis-Napoléon restraining
the conservative drivers of
the engine of reaction.

5 *Economic life: a crisis of confidence*

Everybody is worried about the crisis of 1852. . . . Crops are fetching rotten prices. The tenants won't pay up because they cannot sell their corn without ruining themselves. The poor landowners are penniless and see their property going down in value every day.

General des Salles, in a letter to General Pelissier, 15 March 1851.

[In the Lyon area] . . . there is less and less work all the time. Poverty is widespread. The democrats take advantage of this to stir up trouble. The situation is kept under very active surveillance, and I am ready for anything.

Maréchal de Castellane, *Journal*, entry under 26 March 1851.

6 *Radical Republican appeal to small property owners and workers*

The right to work must be officially recognized, for it is the right to live.

Credit and necessary equipment must be made available to all. For this is the means to a livelihood.

Idlers and parasites must no longer prevent the worker from consuming his products.

. . . Do not assume that the countryside will be dominated, as in the past, by what used until quite recently to be called the big landowners. The big landowners! And who are they, pray? There is hardly more than one owner left in France, and that is capital! And there is only one form of feudalism left: the foul, hateful, all-consuming feudalism of usury.

From *La Révolution*, 17 September 1851.

27 *Talk of Revolution*

France is in peril. The poor classes are deprived of their birth-right, and the rich have ensured that they alone have all the privileges. This state of affairs must not be allowed to continue; by joining together loyally we must create a powerful force in the land. That is the object of the network of clubs covering all France. At a signal, which we are waiting for, we shall all rise up like one man. In a quarter of an hour the Revolution will be complete, the provisional government proclaimed, and the Red flag will be flying on all public buildings.

A spy's report on a speech made before a secret society at
Berlon (Hérault). It was sent along with a report by the
Procureur-général at Montpellier, 9 September 1851.

In 1852, at the first vote, they will rise up and urge the electors excluded by the law of 31 May to force their way into the polling stations.

Report (undated; of autumn 1851) on the plans of a
secret society in Grenoble, by the prefect of the Isère.

. . . Every day they sang songs, many of the words of which are seditious. In one of them the following passage occurs:
> The Red Republic, yes,
> We'll get it,
> With our daggers in our hands . . .

Report by the Procureur-général at Grenoble, 25 August
1851 (Archives nationales BB^{30} 394).

An individual under interrogation claimed that: On a certain day in the near future the parish priests were going to be made prisoner, the churches were to be taken over, and a peal would be rung on the bells. At this signal the members living in the country were supposed to go to the lawyer's offices and burn up all the contracts. After that they would start looting and burning up papers belonging to the aristocrats.

Report by the Procureur-général at Orléans,
11 November 1851 (ibid.).

8 Official credence of the threat of Revolution

It appears likely that the secret society called the Jeune Montagne does exist almost everywhere in France and that is has a central office with three members in Paris and even a European committee in London.

Report (undated) from the prefect of the Var (ibid.).

Paris: The leaders of the clubs have set up in each *arrondissement* a centre whose delegates form the socialist Revolutionary government. This is in permanent contact with the refugees in Switzerland and London.

A large number of reports mention the existence in Paris of a steering committee which is alleged to be in contact with most of the clubs in the departments.

Colmar: In Alsace the secret societies conduct their affairs almost in broad daylight. The steering committee has its headquarters in the offices of the opposition newspaper, which receives encouragement from Paris and provides impetus in this locality by means of its daily articles. It also ensures that its ideas get widely talked about by displaying posters in cafés and public houses. The rural communes are associated; these links are fostered by municipal councillors, or by the officers of the national guard who belong to the extremist party.

Ministry of justice: *Résumé des documents judiciaires:*
Travail sur le mouvement démagogique anterieur–au
2 décembre (ibid.).

9 Republicans: excuses for inaction and promise of action

To be sure, we should deplore the need for a passive attitude in the face of the audacious attacks made by our adversaries. But that is the price of our success in 1852. While defending right with all our power and while protesting against violence, we have to check our noble, but imprudent, impatience; we have to discipline our courage, to help people endure shame and oppression for a time. We have to contain and concentrate all our energies, all our desire for action, all our Revolutionary feeling. We have somehow to dam up all our Republican ardour so that we can let it flood over all at once, on a single day, everywhere.

From *Le National*, 2–3 November 1851.

Everyone is waiting, everyone is worried ... preoccupied, disturbed. That watchword of the enemies of the Republic goes up:
   'The barbarians are at the gates!'
1852 is striding on ...
   We, Republicans and socialists, wait for 1852 calmly, joyfully. 1789 and 1852 are two dates which are linked and joined together. ... Today two great parties confront each other: the Republic of '93, with all its natural corollaries, and the monarchy.

From *La Révolution*, 17 September 1851.

Socialism has invaded the towns and countryside. ... The 1852 elections, conducted under universal suffrage, will unquestionably fill the chamber with the most thorough-going Republicans, the most audacious socialists.

Ibid., 18 October 1851.

30 *The Imperial pretender*

France neither wishes for a return to the old order of things, in no matter what form that may be disguised, nor for ventures into dangerous and impractical utopianism. It is because I am the most natural enemy of both these alternatives that France has given me its confidence. ... Indeed, if my government has not been able to bring about all the improvements it had in mind, that must be blamed on the devious conduct of the various factions. For three years, as you will have noted, I have always had the support of the assembly when it has been a question of combating disorder by repressive measures. But, whenever I have wanted to do good and improve conditions for the people, the assembly has denied me its support.

Speech delivered by Louis-Napoléon at Dijon in May 1851
(in E. Ténot, *Paris en Décembre 1851*).

31 *The Red spectre*

The French nation has ceased to exist. There are, on the old soil of the Gauls, worried rich men and voracious poor ones, and that is all. The poor, trained to be envious, to hate and to lust for loot, are ready in their millions to ravage the châteaux and the mansions, ready to destroy, with one long scream, everything they take to be an insult. What is holding them back at present is the army. . . . The conflict is between order and chaos. . . . It is not you who represent order, you, the bourgeois class of the Revolution. It is the armed forces alone that symbolize it – the army. That is the source of order, and that is the sole order in which you can take comfort. But know – so that you can, under its protection, enjoy your goods that today are threatened and enjoy that sweet repose which is now beginning to seem so desirable – know that you will have to cast to the four winds and for ever the deceitful catechism that the eighteenth-century thinkers taught. You will have to give up all claims to govern. Between the kingdom of the sabre and that of the firebrand you no longer have any choice. Thank God that nineteenth-century sabres are not the sabres of Tamburlain! They are drawn now, not to destroy, but to protect. They have become the civilizing force, for its enemy is barbarism. . . . As for the soldiers' leader, his task is simple. He must resolutely make himself a total dictator.

M. A. Romieu, *La Spectre Rouge de 1852*.

2 *Call for a preventive* coup d'état

The demagogues assert that: We must remain within the bounds of legality. . . . But this legality – everybody replies that that is where the danger lies. . . .

Indeed, what good does this legality do us? In 1852 it will give us two elections at the same time, for the assembly and for the president of the Republic. It gives us those under the feeble protection of the two powers that are now dying, under a law that is contested and in the face of terrifying organization by all the forces of socialism. Those are the safeguards we are offered. We ask whether there is any solution of any sort, from whatever source it may come, of which the dangers are not infinitely surpassed by the dangers of that sort of legality.

From *Le Constitutionnel*, 27 August 1851.

3 *Conservatives await the* coup d'état

Dinner was not very cheerful. Molé pulled an awful face as he talked about the *coup d'état* which is everybody's preoccupation. Molé's view is that there is no course open to the assembly except dignified withdrawal. He repeated his aphorism 'it is better to go out by the door than through the window'. . . . All more or less sensed that the president has beaten the assembly, for the latter no longer enjoys any esteem at all in the country. . . . Taken all in all, everybody is very sad and very worried about the confusion we are in, and nobody sees how we shall get out of it again.

R. Apponyi, *Journal*, entry under 1 December 1851.

Part Five
Coup d'état

Only a small group of men actually organized the coup d'état; *but it satisfied most conservative Notables, who were hoping for greater security. They would not resist it, and neither would the mass of politically indifferent people to whom the legend that went with the name of Bonaparte at least promised national glory and national prosperity. Those who resisted were Republican idealists, supported by peasants and artisans organized in secret societies and prepared to defend, not the conservative Republic, but the new Republic which was to be created following* démocrate-socialiste *victories in the presidential and general elections due in 1852; a Republic which, they had been promised, would institute democratic and social reforms. The failure of isolated uprisings in rural areas was inevitable; the insurgents melted away once military forces were concentrated against them.*

1 Early justifications

PROCLAMATION BY THE PRESIDENT OF THE REPUBLIC

. . . The present situation cannot continue. Each day that passes increases the country's dangers. The assembly, supposed to be the staunchest support of order, has become a hot-bed of sedition. The patriotism of three hundred members was not enough to curb its fatal tendencies. Instead of legislation for the public good, it is forging weapons for civil war. It is making a bid for the power which I wield directly by virtue of the people's will. It fosters every wicked passion. It is jeopardizing the stability of France. I have dissolved the national assembly and I invite the whole people to adjudicate between it and me.

2 December 1851 (Archives nationales F^{1a} 10).

TO PREVENT A CONSERVATIVE COUP?

I haven't time to tell you any details about the Revolution of 2 December, for it is a real one. MM. Changarnier, Thiers, Cavaignac, Lamoricière, Bedeau, Charras, Le Flô, Baze and the rest[1] were plotting openly. The president and his ministers were to be arrested and imprisoned at Vincennes, then impeached and so on, on 3 or 4 December. I was sharper and quicker than those gentlemen.

General de Saint-Arnaud, minister of war, in a letter to
General Pelissier, 5 December 1851.

[1] All were leaders of Conservative opposition to the president in the assembly.

2 *Measures of repression*

THE BUREAUCRACY

All justices of the peace, mayors and other appointees whose support cannot be counted on are to be replaced immediately.

Instructions telegraphed to the prefects from M. Morny, minister of the interior, 2 December 1851 (in Archives nationales F^{1a} 10).

MUTUAL AID SOCIETIES

Pretending to be friendly societies for mutual aid, they existed only to spread the most detestable doctrines.

Circular from the prefect of the Saône-et-Loire to sub-prefects and mayors, 9 January 1852 (ibid.).

CAFÉS AND CABARETS

If one of these establishments becomes a meeting place for these partisans of disorder, if it degenerates into a club or a hot-bed of political propaganda . . . I shall have no hesitation in ordering it to be closed down.

Circular from the prefect of the Saône-et-Loire, 9 January 1852 (ibid.).

THE PRESS

Of prefects and deputy prefects: I have called on them to pay special heed to the press and to ensure that it is kept on a very tight rein. According to the instructions I have given, the newspapers should merely report the facts without indulging in any discussion or hostile comment. Any infraction will entail the immediate suppression of the paper and the imprisonment of the author of the article.

Report from the general officer commanding the 6th subdivision of the 1st military division, 4 December 1851 (Archives historiques du Ministère de la Guerre F^1 51).

3 *Reactions to the* coup

He [Louis-Napoléon] wishes to found a government as religious as that of the Restoration, as prosperous as that of the July monarchy, as grandiose as that of the Emperor, and as virtuous as a Republic must be.

Circular letter from the prefect of the Saône-et-Loire, 6 December 1851 (Archives nationales F^{1a} 10).

On Sunday last the foundry workers of Hayange paraded a bust of the President through the streets in triumph.

Report by the prefect of the Moselle, 8 December 1851
(ibid., F[7] 12654).

The working-class population of Mulhouse and the other industrial centres greeted the news from Paris unemotionally. Production in the workshops was not interrupted for a single hour.

Report from the prefect of the Haut-Rhin, 6 December
1851 (ibid.).

In general the inhabitants of the countryside and even the towns welcome the Revolution which has just taken place. There is no interruption to employment, and assurances have been given to the workers that many recent orders will give them an excellent livelihood for a long time to come.

Report from the general officer commanding the 5th
subdivision of the 1st military division at Rouen,
8 December 1851 (Archives historiques du Ministère de la
Guerre F[1] 52).

Basically the situation does not seem too bad to me. The peasants are delighted by the events of 2 December. But the Reds are pretty active in certain places. The most ridiculous rumours are going round about Paris, Marseilles, even Lyon and this department. I have given orders to the sub-prefects and the *gendarmerie* that people who spread false reports are to be taken into custody at once.

Report by the prefect of the Isère, 9 December 1851 (ibid.).

4 Resistance in Paris

Barricade building has started in the Rue Rambuteau, at the intersection of Rue St Denis and Rue St Martin. Vehicles have been stopped and some omnibuses toppled over. The shout 'To arms!' has been raised at the corner of Rue Grenetat. The general rallying point is at present the St Martin area. It seems certain that a gang of selected activists will be called out under arms on the Carré St Martin around 5 o'clock and that the leaders of this gang have announced that it is a question of an attack of the president's residence. There are rumours of the deaths of Charras and General Bedeau.

There are also claims that patriots are arriving from Rouen and that Ledru-Rollin is in the faubourgs.

Report by the Paris prefect of police to the minister of war, 3 December 1851 (ibid. F^1 51).

Paris is quiet. The barricades that were erected last night were removed without difficulty.

Report from the Armée de Paris, 4 December 1851 (ibid.).

5 *Success of the* coup *in Paris*

I saw quite clearly here what happened, though, very fortunately for France, the national guard did not defend itself. . . .

What is certain is that the unpopularity of the chamber, the surprise and the remarkable way the arrests were all timed to take place at the same moment – the attitude of the army, too, perhaps – meant that in the end nothing very nasty happened. . . . You know, moreover, that those gentlemen [the deputies] were arrested without any show of resistance and conveyed to the Orsay barracks. From there they were transferred by night to Mont Valérien, Mazas and Vincennes. . . . Several who were not taken into custody – M. de la Rochejaquelein, M. de Panat, M. Dufaure – did what they could to get arrested too. But they were informed that orders had been given that they should be left to go free. That made them furious. It was only the next day that the authorities got round to getting rid of all these prisoners by stating that they were going to be transferred to other prisons and then turning them out on the Place Louis XV and in other parts of the city.

[The general feeling was] at first one of amazement, then of annoyance and discontent among the bourgeoisie and the Legitimist and Orléanist aristocracy. Among the workers – indifference, almost approbation. These last few days the bourgeoisie has rallied because of the sustained energy shown by the government, the suppression of the press, and the reports of disgraceful excesses committed by insurgents in several departments. At Poligny Mme Jarry, wife of the sub-prefect, was raped seventeen times. In a castle near Lapalice they forced the lady of the house and her three daughters, all very beautiful, to strip naked and wait on them at table. It is hardly necessary to add that at dessert the citizens shared them in best democratic fashion. It is said that generally they forced their victims to drink champagne so that they would to some extent appear willing accomplices in their brutality. And have you heard about a wretched cavalry

N.C.O. who was butchered near Auch? He was found with his eyes and nails torn out.

Whatever the truth may be about certain details, the fact remains that frightful atrocities have been committed.[1] If the President had not, fortunately for the country and for Europe, taken this energetic and intelligent decision which he has carried off so remarkably well, we were sure to go through a frightful and shocking period in 1852, and its consequences would have been incalculable.

Raymond de Breda, staff captain in the Paris national
guard, in a letter to General Pelissier, 14 December 1851.

6 *Preventive measures*

Only the fervent socialists appear discontented. But they dare not make any move, for they know well that they will be swept aside by the battalion of the 18th line regiment and by the *gendarmerie*.

Report by the officer commanding the *gendarmerie* in the
Haute-Loire, 5 December 1851 (Archives historiques de
Ministère de la Guerre F^1 51).

7 *The* coup *at Lyon*

8 A.M.   At Lyon, according to police reports, the secret societies first went into permanent session. Then the meeting of the Croix-Rousse and Guillotière broke up, because there were not enough people to attend. They explained away their lack of action by saying: 'The president is giving us back universal suffrage. So why should we fight? We shall rely on the polls.'

11 P.M.   I received fresh information from the police. The democrats who had planned to meet in the Pâté de la Grenette and in the nearby squares and streets have just had orders to go back home. The explanation lies in the fact that a great number of democrats failed to appear. As a consequence of the steps taken to put down any attempted insurrection, they did not dare come to the appointed meeting place.

Maréchal de Castellane, *Journal*, entry under 3 December
1851.

[1] These atrocity stories were not true, but they served to strengthen Conservative support for the *coup*.

8 Resistance to the coup

RESISTANCE IN THE LIMOUSIN

According to information from a reliable source the advance on Limoges due to take place in the night of 6/7 December was linked with a plan for a general uprising in the Haute-Vienne and in part of Creuse. It had been settled in advance by the leading demagogues in the city. The reports from the *gendarmerie* describe how emissaries from the democratic committee had gone to give the signal for this general uprising in the countryside. The ringleaders of the Reds were spotted as they prepared for the insurrection. A few arrests took place, and no trouble was sparked off.

The demagogic party was scared by the vigorous counter-measures taken against any attempt at disorder. It may be assumed that there will be no repetition of such a demonstration. . . .

Report by the general officer commanding the 13th
military division, 10 December 1851 (Archives
historiques du Ministère de la Guerre F^1 52).

AT MONTPELLIER

In general, the decent people have refrained from all comments and all demonstrations over the news. But the Reds showed their excitement at once by unwonted activity. A great number of leaders from around Montpellier were summoned to the city and reported at once. . . . All the demagogues from Montpellier and round about were there, numbering some four hundred. All were arrested. But the police picked out the main ringleaders, and they alone were taken into custody.

The soldiers acted with great vigour and remarkable spirit.

Report by the general officer commanding the 7th, 8th,
and 9th military divisions at Montpellier, 3 December 1851
(ibid. F^1 51).

AT GRENOBLE

The members of the Montagnard commission, the members of the administrative Revolutionary commission of Grenoble: an administrative Revolutionary commission composed of several former municipal councillors and twelve of our members is sitting in permanent session. Before calling on the people to take up arms, it is waiting for reports from Lyon and Paris. If insurrection has broken out in those cities, we shall take up arms.

Organize; arrange demonstrations; seize all the officials; replace them, once you know the insurrection has begun at Lyon.

Proclamation dispatched by the prefect of the Isère along
with his report of 9 December 1851 (ibid. F^1 52).

Meeting of 12 municipal councillors: The members of this meeting claimed that the constitution had been violated, that they possessed the right to direct public affairs, that the authorities had forfeited their rights by virtue of article 68 of the constitution, and finally, that resistance was required of every good citizen.

Report by the officer commanding the *gendarmerie* at
Bayonne; undated, but 3 or 4 December 1851 (ibid.
F^1 51).

IN THE SAÔNE-ET-LOIRE

[*In the Theatre at Tournos*] . . .

We found two or three hundred people grouped round a table. On it stood M. Burot, a café proprietor, reading the constitution aloud. The commissioner of police called upon them to go back home. They replied that they were the sovereign people and that, since the constitution had been violated, nobody had the right to prevent them holding a meeting. They refused any longer to recognize us as representatives of the executive, since the latter had no authority save that derived from the people. 'To the Hôtel-de-Ville', they cried and at once marched off in that direction.

Report from the officer commanding the *gendarmerie* at
Tournos (Saône-et-Loire), 4 December 1851 (ibid.).

9 Waiting on Paris

Last night about seven o'clock, a thousand to twelve hundred persons in overalls gathered at the railway waiting for news from Paris. Their attitudes, without being exactly threatening, indicated fairly plainly that they were not supporters of order. Most of these men had come in from the country.

Report from the officer commanding the *gendarmerie* at
Dijon, 4 December 1851 (ibid.).

10 Insurrection and revolt

IN THE VAR

The demagogues' system is to form groups in several different communes and to march together on other communes where the supporters of law and order are in a majority. By threats and intimidation they break up the municipal councils and set up a commission, selecting its members from among themselves or from their supporters in the commune in question.

Report by the officer commanding the *gendarmerie* in the Var; from Draguignon, 6 December 1851 (ibid. F^1 52).

A column of around five thousand rebels with cannon coming from the direction of Le Digne made contact near Oraison with a battalion of the 14th Light Infantry. After two hours' fighting, this battalion had to fall back on Vinon (Var). It lost a few men and killed many of the enemy.

Report by the general officer commanding the 7th military division, 11 December 1851 (Archives nationales F^7 12654).

IN THE ALLIER

I am still receiving fresh news from Donjon (Allier). It sounds more and more alarming. At 9 p.m. the church bells were still ringing there and in the neighbouring communes. The roads are blocked by barricades. People are coming in from the countryside armed with scythes and forks. . . .

Those who turn out to support the authorities are disarmed and driven away. The Notables are being arrested and held prisoner like the detachment of *gendarmerie*.

Report by the general officer commanding the 5th subdivision of the 13th military division; midnight 4 December 1851 (Archives historiques du Ministère de la Guerre F^1 51).

AT BÉZIERS

On 4 December last, the town of Béziers woke amid the horrors of civil war; after a night of apparent calm a formidable insurrection burst out in its very midst. Six thousand determined men entered the city, marching in an orderly fashion under the command of their leaders. All were armed with muskets, pistols, sabres, scythes with the handle fitted back to front, crowbars, iron forks sharpened so they could be used as weapons, cutlasses on the end of sticks, daggers and many other murderous weapons thought up by the ferocious men taking part in the insurrection.

A certain number of bourgeois swathed in burnouses had mingled with the groups. Among the men, some were in their working clothes and most were wearing overalls, but others were dressed in rags and had blackened faces. Nearly all had red sashes around their heads or waists. The leaders wore their sashes over one shoulder and across the chest.

Evidence of Commandant Bourelly at the second court
martial of the 10th military division, sitting at Montpellier;
reported in *Gazette des Tribunaux*, 29–30 March 1852.

In the morning before it was light armed bands from all the neighbouring countryside – some led by flags and drums, others slipping into the city in separate groups – formed a column of fifteen hundred to two thousand persons. About 6.30 a.m. it made its way to the sub-prefect's residence. . . . The armed band that had come from the direction of the Hôtel-de-Ville advanced, waving sashes and flags and calling the soldiers their brothers. . . . Eventually a shot was fired; the troops riposted. After the first volley seven or eight rebels fell mortally wounded. The band fell back when the soldiers fired, but the insurgents continued to shoot as they retreated, taking cover under the walls and in doorways. The struggle lasted nearly an hour.

Report by the officer commanding the *gendarmerie* in the
Hérault; from Béziers, 5 December 1851 (Archives
historiques du Ministère de la Guerre F^1 51).

IN THE LOT-ET-GARONNE
Marmande and Ville-neuve are still in the hands of the insurgents. Armed bands have threatened Agen, but have not dared force their way in. I am waiting for reinforcements before proceeding at once to stern measures.

Report by the prefect of the Lot-et-Garonne, 5 December
1851 (Archives nationales F^7 12654).

ROLE PLAYED BY NATURAL CONDITIONS
As for the Department of the Hautes Alpes, it is under snow, and I have absolutely no worries about the area. . . .

Report by the general officer commanding the 7th military
division, 8 December 1851 (Archives historiques du
Ministère de la Guerre F^1 52).

REASONS FOR INSURRECTION
. . . You cannot take into custody three-quarters of the population of a department, and it is perhaps no exaggeration to fix these proportions

between those who have, to a greater or lesser degree, taken part in the activities of the secret societies and those who refrained from doing so.

In the Nièvre there are many reasons for disorder. The first that needs stressing is the vast amount of landed property belonging to the great families. It is let out to tenants, sub-tenants and share-croppers while the owners are far away. Their absenteeism and remoteness removes all possible influence or chance of moral guidance. The second factor is the great mass of workers employed in industrial enterprises and on the railways.

In several localities there exist causes of poverty and anxiety about material well-being which must naturally tend to leave the populations a prey to evil passions. . . . It is easy to be honest and moral while you are enjoying to the full every good thing and all the pleasures of life.

Report by the general officer commanding the 2nd
subdivision of the 19th military division, from the area of
Nevers and Clamency (Nièvre), 9 January 1852 (Archives
nationales F⁷ 12710).

ORGANIZATION

Before the promulgation of the decree of 2 December last, the mood and political climate in the four departments that make up this judicial province was deteriorating daily under the evil influence of socialist propaganda. This was put out cleverly and persistently. The vast network of secret societies was spreading day by day, and, with rare exceptions, all the communes of Gard, Ardèche and Vaucluse had already allowed themselves to be enmeshed.

Things had come to such a pass that the more decent peasants, those least open to suspicion on account of their previous records, ended up by agreeing, when you discussed the events of 1852 with them, they had no choice but to stand shoulder to shoulder with the other members of their class if there was an insurrection and vote in the elections just like them.

[In the Gard] the objective of the insurrection was to surprise the town of Nîmes in the course of the night of 5/6 December with large columns of peasants. . . . A large proportion of the population, which had for a long time been familiar with the idea of insurrection (thanks to contact with secret societies) responded only too gladly to the rallying cry. . . . The columns were marching on Nîmes armed in revolutionary fashion, that is to say, with muskets stolen from the town halls, sporting guns, scythes, pitchforks and sticks.

But for the immense influence exerted by these secret societies, the very attempt to raise an insurrection would have been impossible. It was because of the daily contacts between committees in the chief town of the Department and those in the *arrondissements*, *cantons* and communes that it was possible to mobilize these armed masses in the space of only forty-eight hours.

[At Vauvert – *arrondissement* Nîmes, Gard] . . . A secret society was founded under the name 'Workers' club'. . . . This society split into two as a result of dissension within; one section was called the Girondin society, the other the Montagnard society. When the time for action came they were supposed to join forces. They received their political instructions from the leaders of the socialist committee set up in Nîmes. The latter often went to Vauvert to preach the most subversive doctrines. The object of the members was the setting up of a democratic, social Republic after the overthrow of the government of Louis-Napoléon by armed force. They were all supposed to rise up at the first signal from their chiefs. They had adopted the red flag as party emblem. Their monthly subscription was twenty-five centimes. The initiation ceremony involved making an oath, with your hand on the daggers, to obey the leaders blindly and never to reveal the society's secrets.

Report by the Procureur-général at Nîmes, 27 January 1852 (ibid. BB^{30} 396).

ACCUSED: I was admitted into the secret society in April 1850 at Béziers, along with seven others from Capestang. They made me help with recruiting.

Q. What was the form of words used at admission?
R. We were made to swear we would defend the Republic in every way and everywhere.
Q. But what were the objectives of this society?
R. Its aim was to spread by all legal means the principles of the Republic. Any man who was admitted was expected to agree to total self-denial. Every other consideration had to be disregarded when the society made its demands. The Montagnards were supposed above all to be deeply democratic and to help one another.
Q. Was there not talk of socialism?
R. Never.
Q. But you know perfectly well that in the society there were men who wanted private property to be divided out.
R. I do agree that there were things that were wrong in the society. Among the members there were people whose conduct was not beyond reproach.
Q. Were you not treasurer of this society?
R. Yes, sir; I collected the subscriptions.

Q. Did you not send money to Béziers?

R. No, never. Never to my knowledge was this money used for political purposes. I always thought the money was to be used for welfare purposes.

Q. Had the secret society designated a place where the members should gather if circumstances required?

R. Yes. It was the place called Lisle. All the orders came from Béziers. . . .

Q. What have you to say about the events of 4 December?

R. We learned the news of the dissolution of the assembly when the mayor read the proclamation in the evening of 3 December. Emissaries from Béziers arrived at 11 o'clock. . . . The executive committee had discussions with them.

Q. Is it true that, after the gendarmes had been rendered powerless, you led your column into a field where you said that a roll-call should be taken and that all those who were not present should be shot?

R. I was anxious to keep those people all together and I did threaten any who slipped away with severe punishment. But I do not think that I said they would be shot. . . .

Q. So you did know that there were in the bands certain men who wanted to start looting and who were capable of taking the opportunity to pay off old scores?

R. I did hear it said that there were such men. That is why I wanted to keep them together in a group. People like that are not used to discipline, and it is very difficult to keep control of them. I think I did a good job for Capestang that day.

Q. Did you not at carnival time lend your mule so that it could carry round an effigy clad in white?

R. No, sir.

Q. Did people thrust a lance through this several times, as if to represent what was going to happen in 1852?

R. I had no part in it, if that did happen.

Proceedings of the second court martial of the 10th
military division sitting at Montpellier: the trial of
Maxime Chambert, forty-four-year-old carter and
peasant; reported in *Gazette des Tribunaux*, 9 April 1852.

I agreed to join the secret society for fear of losing my job as a postman in the country. But that didn't come off, because I lost it. I witnessed the meeting of the executive commission in Donadieu's house. Chambert, Roux, Jean Pech, Grimal and Andre-Pierre Chucasse were present. There were also two emissaries from Béziers. They had brought an order. Roughly what it said was: 'Article 68 of the constitution. The president of the Republic, since he has dissolved the chambers, should be pursued and put to death.'

The witness declares that he had heard it said by members of the society that in 1852 everybody would be rich and that property would be shared. out to all.

The same: trial of Antoine Mauril, peasant; 12–13 April 1852.

Q.   How could a man of your age, a man of experience, an old man, in fact, be so thoughtless as to join secret societies?
R.   I did see, once I had been admitted, that I had done the wrong thing. But it wasn't easy to get out again. Before your initiation they made lots of promises. Afterwards they made lots of threats.

The same: trial of Isaac Lauze, sixty-one-year-old weaver; 27 May 1852.

Q.   You are accused of having belonged to secret societies, conspiring, and suborning soldiers. What have you to say in your defence?
R.   Let me explain very frankly. In March or April 1851 we left for Montelimart. At that date, Sergeant Brunot had been admitted to a secret society at Lyon. We stayed a month at Montelimart and from there we went back to Valence. In that city we had some conversations about politics with Brunot and Bonfils. With no delay my company was sent off on detachment to Graves in the *arrondissement* of Crest. In this new garrison Bonfils came to see me. He persuaded me to go for a walk with him. He told me that Brunot had signed him up in a secret society at Valence, as well as Sergeant Piel. He added that nearly all the N.C.O.s and soldiers in the company were members, that I was the only one who wasn't, and that I couldn't be odd man out. . . . He predicted that there would be a terrible Revolution and that I should get rid of all my fears, since these societies did not keep any written records and that, even if the Democratic party had the worst of it, all evidence of guilt would disappear and never appear in a court. He added that if at that fatal moment there were to be an engagement between troops and the inhabitants of any locality, the people would not fire at us and we would shoot over their heads. I turned down this approach.

The next day Bonfils suggested going for another walk. Just as we were going into M. Benoît's property we met Brunot and Perrier. Several minutes later, just as we were going back into the billets, in a dark and lonely place, one of the pair said to me: 'We have brought you to this house so that you can be admitted to the society by a certain person. He has been very hurt by your refusal. As for us, we are anxious because you may give away our secret.' And putting their hands on the hilts of their sabres they said to me that they would rather stab me to the heart than let go unpunished any word of accusation spoken against them. On bended knee I vowed to keep silent.

On Corpus Christi Day Bonfils again invited me to take a walk with him. I agreed. With us were also Sirot, Piel and Perrier. Arriving in quite a secluded spot Perrier said to me: 'We have allowed you long enough to think it over. You must agree to join now.' They called me so many names that I agreed to join their society.

The day I was admitted they first made me kneel down. Then they blindfolded us. Next we had to state our surnames, forenames and occupations in a loud voice. We were informed that we were going to swear on the questions that would be put to us.

Previously they had taken away our sabres, and lances were pointed at our chests. Perrier, who admitted us, said he had also been delegated for this by the central society at Lyon, and addressed us as follows: 'Do you swear to pour out your life-blood for the liberty of the country.' 'I swear so to do.' 'To avenge those who have been martyred for the cause of liberty.' 'I swear so to do.' 'To avenge the Montagnards who have been deported.' 'I swear so to do.' 'Never to betray the secrets of the society.' 'I swear so to do.' 'What does a traitor deserve?' 'He deserves death.'

A dagger was suspended over the chests of the men being admitted. Once this form of words has been gone through, the new member is helped to his feet, everyone embraces him and he is told that the members have secret recognition. You have to hold out the first finger of the left hand, with the remainder held tight, pointing to the right side of the left eye, raising it and lowering it. The man you make the signal to replies by grasping with his thumb and the first two fingers of the left hand the left side of the brim of his hat, with his thumb beneath, the first two fingers on top, and the others curled up. Then the two members approach. They have also three watchwords which are 'Hope, Patience and Perseverance'. The man who gives the signal pronounces the first word, the other replies with the second, then the first gives the third watchword. Then you ask if the other is a member of the society and each promises to help spread the word.

In the course of June we were taken to see a gentleman who was supposed to be very rich. It was M. Larger. It was said he had been a colonel in the Paris national guard. At the time he was managing the estates of M. Crémieux, the lawyer.

We went into a silkworm cocoonery where we found Larger and Joubert. The room was small and there were a lot of us. They sent for some bread and wine. Soon Larger asked Joubert whether the doors of the house were well guarded. On receiving an affirmative reply, Larger asked Joubert whether he wished to address us. Gradually becoming more and more animated he told us he was the delegate of the Montagne. He described the lot of the people most vividly, explaining that they wanted for bread, that it was at last time to proclaim the independence of the people and that the alarm trumpet should now be sounded. He spoke to us in general terms about the men dedicated to the holy cause of the freedom of the peoples. He portrayed them as martyrs shedding their life's blood in 1848 and being condemned to transportation. He quoted Robespierre as one of these martyrs and, comparing the revolution of '93 with the one that he wished to bring about, he said, 'Ours will be more terrible'; and speaking directly to us, the soldiers, he added, 'Don't be stopped by bloodshed. You will have to kill everything that shows any resistance. . . .' Then, on the subject of the President of the Republic, he represented him as a head of state who crushed the people with taxes to pay for his petty, personal pleasures. He told us we were not stuffed dummies and that, in the new state of affairs, there would not be an army any more, since everybody would be a soldier. As for his language, it was marked by his use of foul, disgusting expressions.

Proceedings of the second court martial of the 6th
military division, sitting at Lyon: trial of Simon Dudrage,
twenty-five-year-old sergeant in the 13th infantry
regiment; reported in *Gazette des Tribunaux*, 6 June 1852.

ACCUSED: I joined the secret society in the hope that if we were ill – my little daughter or me, that is – we'd get help. On 4 December my section leader stopped me from going to work.
Q. What reason did he give you?
R. Well, to tell you the truth, I think he told me that it was to celebrate Louis-Napoléon's birthday (*laughter in court*), and that there was a meeting.

Proceedings of the second court martial of the 10th
military division sitting at Montpellier: trial of Etienne
André, forty-eight-year-old peasant; reported in *Gazette
des Tribunaux*, 10 April 1852.

THE PRISONER: I was recruited by Maxime Chambert[1] in the café owned by Louis Rey (one of the accused men). I had been told that this society would provide help for people who were ill or in difficulties. We had been promised the right to work.

Ibid.: trial of François Caumette, thirty-five-year-old
peasant.

[1] See p. 165.

Ponsier, a gardener, said to the workers: 'You took no part in the insurrection. You'll be butchered. As for me, now I don't have to ask any more: I just take possession of the garden I used to lease. And while you poor blighters will have the cabbage stalks to eat, I shall have the heart.' (*Laughter in court.*)

Ibid.: evidence given by François Colombier, gardener, concerning events at Bédarieux (Hérault); 7–8 June 1852.

ACCUSED: . . . I was admitted into a secret society . . . but I never heard any talk of looting or arson or paying off old scores. We had been promised the right to work. They threatened to kill me if I went to work as normal so I reported to the meeting place with my musket.

Ibid.: trial of Marcel Lignon, twenty-two-year-old peasant; 10 April 1852.

As a member of a secret society I had to march with them because my life was threatened. My mother was in tears and went all the way to the Place de l'Abreuvoir with me. She wanted to make me go home again. But Donadieu and Claude Poursines threatened her.

Ibid.: evidence of Prosper Fous, proprietor.

A dozen armed men turned up at the factory. They were looking for one of my workmen who had failed to turn out when called for. The worker refused to join them. He even said, 'You're just a rabble. It's true I joined your society. But that wasn't so I could go around looting and murdering. You took me in!' There was some talk of shooting him.

Ibid.: evidence of Dominique Ramy, director of the gasworks at Bédarieux; 17 June 1852.

Q.   Did you not threaten to kill one Bigot?
R.   There was no political motive for that. I wanted to kill Bigot because I'd discovered he was trying to get friendly with my wife. But later on I gave up the plan.

Ibid.: trial of Jean Pech, twenty-six-year-old peasant; 10 April 1852.

The accused does not seem endowed with normal intelligence. He speaks only in patois.

ACCUSED: I was in the secret society.
Q. Did you not take an oath to defend the Republic? Which Republic?
R. Don't know.
Q. The social Republic?
R. S'pose so. (*Laughter in court.*)

Ibid.: trial of Urban Lignon, twenty-two-year-old peasant.

Q. Why did you get mixed up with the insurrection?
R. The others had been ready to go along. I didn't want to be the odd man out.

Proceedings of the second court martial of the 19th military division sitting at Clamency: trial of Louis-Martin Boudin, nineteen-year-old shoemaker; reported ibid., 16–17 February 1852.

12 Sung defiance

Bugger the kings! Bugger the cossacks!
Hunger is marching today.
The harvest is coming, right soon, right soon,
And we'll sweep all the tyrants away.

Verse of a song found on a man arrested at Saint-Étienne; included with an undated report from the Procureur-général at Lyon (Archives nationales BB^{30} 396).

13 Leaders of insurrection

Emile Maillet
In Bâgé-le-Chatel and its environs he was the head of the extreme demagogic party. He was active in winning recruits to socialism. On account of his influence in the area as a lawyer he made an important contribution to the organization of an armed band which set out from Bâgé-le-Chatel for Mâcon to pillage that town. He went there in order to keep in close touch with events and report to his band all the intelligence he had been able to gather. But hearing that the troops were going to meet them with musket fire, just as they already had done when threatened by another band, he himself turned back without delay. When he made contact with his men a

very short distance from Mâcon he urged them to scatter. They did so, throwing down their arms in the process.

From the register of *Décisions de la Commission militaire superieur de l'Ain* (Archives historiques du Ministère de la Guerre G^8 196).

Antoine Borne
... A doctor, aged forty years. He was always an outstanding figure in the clubs for the violence of his revolutionary speeches and of his attacks on religion and its ministers. He was a member both of the society of 'United Workers of the *Croix-rousse*', and also of the secret societies. . . . A very dangerous man, with great influence over the people.

From a list of prisoners in Lyon awaiting transportation to Algeria (ibid.).

14 Agitators

Beside the demagogues you have to place the more or less convinced democrats who did not want anarchy but who are at present working to lead us in that direction. It is at Troyes above all that men of this complexion are to be found. They were recruited from among the solicitors, lawyers, doctors and shop-keepers.

In the Yonne
The ways of winning them [the people] over varied according to the locality and the individual. In one place people banded together to bring about tax reductions or even the abolition of taxes, especially the liquor tax. In another place the objective was an increase in wages and the re-organization of labour. Elsewhere people were opposed to the reintroduction of unpaid feudal labour and church tithes. .... Some people were promised highly paid sinecures; others were to be absolved of their debts; the tenants were to be given possession of the land which they were farming. ... The passions of every class and age were flattered. But a special effort was made to attract young people between eighteen and twenty. Their inexperience and idealism made them easy to influence.

There was nothing political in the insurrection. Its aim was certainly not the restoration of a constitution which was not viable nor the defence of an assembly whose impotence and lack of unity was becoming more apparent every day. People took up arms for loot, rapine and murder, for every excess and crime that is born of irreligion, hatred of authority and envy of the upper classes; in a word, because of an insatiable desire for material benefits.

... To those known to have some tendency to political passions, they talked of setting up a democratic and social Republic, of the danger to the country. They gave the others to understand that soon their poverty would come to an end, and that it would be their turn to be rich. There were also some who let themselves be persuaded that it was a question merely of a friendly society.

Report by the Procureur-général at Paris, 20 January 1852
(Archives nationales BB³⁰ 396).

[The insurrection] was only the partial, premature execution of a vast plot that should have shaken all France in 1852.... All the communes should have rebelled at the same moment, taken up arms and seized all the administrative centres.

The uprising was social far more than it was political, though among the leaders of the rebellion some thought it was simply a matter of politics, of defending or avenging the constitution. . . . Setting up secret societies was not, for them, a means of spreading the doctrines about social reform in which they believed. It was just a tool for stirring up the lower classes and an instrument of help in forming the revolutionary army that would win a triumph for their party.

No doubt, too, among the insurgents there were some who did not know what it was they were fighting for. There is no lie that would not have been used to provoke evil passions in them. Some thought they were taking up arms in defence of Louis-Napoléon and responding to his appeal. Others were out for a tax cut. . . . Another group imagined it was a question of winning back universal suffrage; there were others who in fact simply gave way to the violent pressure exerted by the more determined who threatened to shoot them if they refused to join in with them.

But, amid these misguided men, there existed in every rebellious commune dangerous ring-leaders who had been warped by socialist doctrines. They were inspired by ferocious instincts and marched resolutely forward toward social revolution. . . . It was not a question for them of a plot because of political hatred; none of these agitators had lost anything or had anything to lose. This was an attack on property. This is what they wanted to revise, modify, transfer. It is Babeuf's plot which they wanted to transform from an insane plan into bloody execution.

... After a few days of power the leaders were overwhelmed by events everywhere. They themselves recognized their incapacity to control those they had led into insurgency. But they had repeated so many times over in the past three years, that the constitution must be defended, if need be with armed force, that they were in their turn obliged to join in because of threats and terror.

Report (undated) by the Procureur-général at Agen,
concerning the departments of Lot-et-Garonne, Gers and
Lot (ibid.).

In spite of prohibitions from the authorities there was in the departments of Rhône, Ain and Loire a positive flood of pamphlets, brochures and handbills. They were aimed at the workers and peasants, attacking them where they were most susceptible, for they were intellectually and emotionally inclined to the damnable notions of socialism. For, in the country, socialism means terrorism – it could not be anything else.

Saint-Simonism, Fouriérism, communism, all the successive versions of socialist ideas made a deep impression on our working-class population. They were found all the more ready to nibble at the bait of sedition because class hatred and antagonism between worker and manufacturer were satisfied by it. For some time, however, the political temperature has been going down in the mutual aid societies. Recently the revolutionary party has turned all its propaganda efforts toward the country districts where terrorist fanaticism could be stirred up.

Report (undated) by the Procureur-général at Lyon
(ibid. BB^{30} 396).

At Lyon the secret societies seem discouraged on account of the arrests. According to the police they no longer dare to hold meetings.

Comte de Castellane, *Journal*, entry under 12 December
1851.

The municipal council of the *Croix-rousse* in this city, which is made up largely of Reds, is so scared that it has, incredibly enough, decided to send out a loyal address and declare its support for the president.

Ibid.: 4 January 1852.

At the present moment nobody wishes to seem approving of what is going on in Paris. But, once the blood-letting is over, the situation will be accepted and, to avoid letting in the Reds, people will rally to the new government.

R. Apponyi, *Journal*, entry under 4 December 1851.

15 *Resistance to the* coup d'état *became its justification*

I am informed by numerous reports that the vast majority of the people who want good order are, no matter what their shade of political opinion, adherents of Prince Louis-Napoléon. For by his energetic measures he has saved them from massacres and looting. A short time back some did not want to believe there was any threat of this. But now they have no doubt on account of the many instances of it seen these last few days.

Report by the officer commanding the 15th legion of *gendarmerie* in the departments of the Gard, Ardèche, Hérault and Lozère, 18 December 1851 (in Archives historiques du Ministère de la Guerre F^1 53).

The president's action has saved the country from the dire calamities that had for long been threatened in 1852. . . . In this connection we have a confession to make. We never did lend much credence to all those grim threats to society. We thought in our naïve way that, apart from the natural excitement of the election, the year 1852 would pass by very quietly. . . . But when we saw the peasants of Var, Ardèche, Basses-Alpes up in insurrection, then we did see the real menace to the country.

From *Courier de Tarn-et-Garonne*, 18 December 1852.

People's minds are in turmoil. Every party seems to understand that it must rally to Prince Louis-Napoléon. Necessity dominates every conviction, and all other allegiances have to be forgotten. The old Conservatives want order at any price. Order resides in the army. The rebellions in the south give great force to these feelings. The social question dominates the political one.

Report by the prefect of the Ille-et-Vilaine, 14 December 1852 (Archives nationales F^7 12654).

The vast majority of the inhabitants, though Legitimists, support the President's action, not out of personal preference, but because they are horrified at the thought of socialism.

Report by the sub-prefect at Ancenis (Loire Inférieure),
5 December 1851 (ibid.).

Dear General,
As you so rightly say, the die is cast. The time for weighing up the odds has gone. Whatever opinion may be adopted about the necessity for the steps that have been taken, all men who are loyal to the country must now hope that power will remain in the hands of the authorities, and that a regular government will be set up in France for at least a few years. The errors of all the parties, those of the national assembly in particular, resulted in the *coup d'état* which was brought off with all the calmness and co-ordination that could be desired.

General de Salles, in a letter to General Pelissier,
12 December 1851.

Events speak for themselves!
Who exactly is in revolt at present?
Who is causing bloodshed in our departments?
Who else but the barbarous militia of the secret societies, that is to say, of communism and terrorism.

The decent folk in all the parties were at first abashed by the astonishing events of 2 December. Yet they have seen the truth of the matter in the sinister glare of the fires and crimes of every description committed by bands of insurgents in Clamecy, Poligny and other places. . . .

Louis-Napoléon Bonaparte, from the supreme position in which he is placed, had seen and judged the situation in France before they had realized what was wrong. Appreciating the magnitude of the peril he has chosen appropriate measures to deal with it.

. . . Now the decent folk in every party are convinced. They recognize that Louis-Napoléon Bonaparte was right to invoke, for the salvation of our land, the *supreme right that comes from the people and the supreme force that comes from God.*

For is it not indeed heaven-sent, the strength of our army which spares us the terrible trials of 1852?

For, once more, what is at stake? What sort of a war is it that is being waged in too many parts of our land?

We repeat: it is a war against communism and terrorism.

That war would have been universal in 1852.

It is only partial and localized in 1851.

A few unhappy cities that were only lightly defended because they have only small populations were the victims of the most deplorable attacks.

In 1852 all France would have been the scene of similar outrages.

And it cannot be said any more that the government's measures provoked the disorders which in fact they were intended to prevent.

That cannot be said. For some of the very people who were recognized opponents of the government are being treated as enemies by the insurgents.

These savage bands are in fact attacking all the parties – Legitimists, Orléanists and moderate Republicans. . . .

It does not make much difference to these looters and bandits, these communist rebels, what opinions are held by people who own something.

These people's crime is to own something, to have a family. As a punishment their property is pillaged, and their wives and daughters raped.

Well, in 1852 France would have been dishonoured by devastation, profanation and murder on a vast scale.

That is what the members of all decent parties appreciate now. A few days ago they were blaming the president of the Republic. Now they are thanking him.

Socialism going off to war with musket and knapsack slung over its shoulder – the musket for killing, the knapsack for loot. That says everything: that explains everything.

Society must rise up against this invasion by savagery. It has a right to do so and a duty to do so. Everywhere the man who wants law and order must stand shoulder to shoulder with the soldier in the defence of civilization. That is the right of society when it is at grips with the infernal claims of barbarism.

From *L'Union*, 30 December 1851.

16 Widespread indifference

The morale of the people is good. They only want peace and quiet. So when they heard of the events in Paris they were alarmed in case their part of the country would be disturbed, not by locals but by various bands originating from the towns.

The entire population is hard working and perfectly calm. It has very little interest in politics. We have no factories to attract workers from outside. Neither do we have any influential people or extremists in any of the parties. . . . As for the political events, nobody mentions them. What you hear said by those who do refer to them is more or less this: 'What does it matter who governs us, provided trade picks up and everything is peaceful. That's what we need.'

Report by a *gendarmerie* officer in the department of the Mayenne, 11 December 1851 (Archives historiques du Ministère de la Guerre F^1 53).

7 Demand for MORAL ORDER

'1852 is dead'. . . . The attitude of sixty-two of the departments showed there is no gainsaying this proud, forceful statement. But the fourteen others held on to everything that socialism had promised them for 1852, and they gave France and the whole civilized world a final and unprecedented warning of what, completely and definitively, Christian society would have become but for the events of 2 December. The terrorism of the Middle Ages . . . the invasions by Visigoths and Vandals, the sacking and pillaging of the richest towns, horrors of every description – all were reproduced, with the additional aggravation that this time the barbarians were our fellow-countrymen.

It was directed by dismissed schoolteachers . . . lawyers without briefs . . . hack writers with whom the Conservative press would have nothing more to do and whose appetites could not be satisfied by the anarchist press . . . by the London committee, by the various meetings of the Montagne, by Swiss and Polish refugees, by old convicts sentenced to transportation, prisoners on Belle-isle, and by the representatives of a few workers' organizations. . . . This army is known about. If not known about, its nature can be guessed at – workers made sullen by idleness and drunkenness, peasants driven into fanaticism by the hope of a fair legal division of the land and of the châteaux and by a general tax repayment, and recidivists, tramps and idlers, envious and ill-educated men; all the scum, in a word.

P. Mayer, *Histoire du Deux Décembre*, 1852.

It is a fact that, as well as our farmers, manufacturers and workers – in a word, all those people who live decent lives of honest toil – there is in our midst a tribe of pariahs, idlers, ne'er-do-wells, men greedy for every luxury, who have deserted their native land to join secret societies and who have made brigandage their social creed.

From *Le Constitutionnel*, 12 December 1851.

18 Plebiscite

To vote against Louis-Napoléon is simply to give in to the socialist Revolution, at present the only possible successor to the government of the day. It is calling in the dictatorship of the Reds to replace the dictatorship of a prince who over the last three years has done incomparable good in the causes of law and order and of Catholicism.

. . . Voting for Louis-Napoléon does not mean approving of everything he has done. It is a question of making a choice between him and the total ruination of France. This is not to say that his government is the one we consider ideal, but just that we would rather have a prince who has displayed resolution and skill than those who nowadays are showing their true colours in murdering and looting. There is no question here of confusing the Catholic cause with that of a party or of a dynasty. It is a matter of arming the temporal powers – the only ones that count today – with the necessary strength to conquer the forces of crime, to defend our homes and altars and to save our wives from men whose lust respects nothing. . . .

We are entering the most difficult stage of our journey toward a real social restoration, the stage when ideas and ethics have to be defended.

M. Montalembert, letter published in *Le Constitutionnel*,
15 December 1851.

[In the department of the Aube, the newspaper] *L'Aube* . . . rallied to the cause of the president of the Republic. It did so, it is true, without enthusiasm, as if giving in to a necessity. The Orléanist convictions of its editor-in-chief did not allow him to change course suddenly, for that would have undermined his reputation. *La Paix* showed less reluctance and made no bones about ceasing to support the Legitimist cause and adopting Bonapartism.

In certain communes [of the Marne] bands and drums celebrated the count of the poll. In others the emperor's bust was paraded through the streets. In one commune where a single 'no' was found in the ballot-boxes the municipal authorities took immediate steps to destroy the voting-slip in order to protect the man responsible for it from the rage of the mob. Attempts were made to identify him by his handwriting.

Report by the Procureur-général at Paris, 20 January 1852
(Archives nationales BB^{30} 396).

Porters from the Paris markets parade in support of Louis-Napoléon.

19 Deo gratias

A solemn *Te Deum* is to be sung in all churches as an act of thanksgiving, to ask for God's blessing on the great mission just confided by the people of France to the president of the Republic and to thank Him for the preservation of France from the threat of anarchy.

From a circular letter despatched by the prefect of the
Maine-et-Loire to sub-prefects and mayors, 2 January
1852 (ibid. F^{1a} 10).

20 *The future?*

When, as a result of these steps, security is solidly re-established, the funds which have been hoarded out of fear will come back into circulation. Credit will be re-established; speculation will dare to play its role again; big business will pick up; long-term operations will start up again because there is no longer any uncertainty about the future. Production will increase, and building will start again. The activity of one industry will have a good effect on the next and this one on the next. Thus business activity will become general.

Declaration by the chamber of commerce of Gray
(Haute-Saône), 10 December 1851 (ibid.).

Louis-Napoléon, the elect of the People, of the Army and of the Clergy.
Popular print reproducing the text of the proclamation of 8 December 1851.

21 Revolution and reaction

What is happening may be defined as follows. The most odious actions of the Revolutionaries have served to feed the hatreds and calm the fears of the Conservative party. You must, indeed, go right back to the committee of public safety and the Terror to find in our history anything like what we can see now. . . . What is heartbreaking is to see the mass of people applauding and feeling it is not being oppressed but is itself oppressor. . . . Nothing shows better the frightful terror into which the violent but, above all, mad-cap Revolution of February has thrown those weak spirits. They were ready to put up with anything cheerfully and even lend a helping hand with anything, provided the spectre of socialism, which troubles their happiness by threatening their future, is banished.

Alexis de Tocqueville, in a letter to Henry Reeve,
9 January 1852.

The Bonaparte dynasty represents not the revolutionary, but the conservative peasant; not the peasant that strikes out beyond the condition of his social existence, the small holding, but rather the peasant who wants to consolidate this holding, not the country folks who, linked up with the towns, want to overthrow the old order through their own energies, but on the contrary those who, in stupefied seclusion within this old order, want to see themselves and their small holdings saved and favoured by the ghost of the empire. . . .

As the executive authority which has made itself an independent power, Bonaparte feels it to be his mission to safeguard 'bourgeois order'. But the strength of this bourgeois order lies in the middle class. He looks on himself, therefore, as the representative of the middle class and issues decrees in this sense. Nevertheless, he is somebody solely due to the fact that he has broken the political power of this middle class and daily breaks it anew. Consequently, he looks on himself as the adversary of the political and literary power of the middle class. But by protecting its material power, he generates its political power anew.

Karl Marx, *The Eighteenth Brumaire of Louis Bonaparte.*

Removal of the inscription Liberté, Egalité et Fraternité from public buildings.

Biographical sketches

BARBÈS, (SIGISMUND AUGUSTE) ARMAND (1809–1870), a leading member of secret societies during the July Monarchy. He participated in the Paris insurrection of May 1839, was imprisoned until the February Revolution, then organized the Société des Droits de l'Homme and the Club de la Révolution. He was colonel of the 12th legion of the national guard. Elected to the constituent assembly by the Aude, he was arrested following the demonstration of 15 May 1848 and imprisoned until the amnesty of 1854. He was then exiled for life.

BARROT, ODILON (1791–1873), a leader of the dynastic Left opposition during the July Monarchy, against the immobilism of Guizot. He was among the organizers of the banquet campaign (1847) for constitutional reform that preceded the February Revolution, and was a minister in the first government of Louis-Napoléon's presidency, before returning to a liberal opposition.

BEAUMONT, GUSTAVE DE (1802–1866), a writer who collaborated with Alexis de Tocqueville. Procureur du roi in 1831, later deputy, then ambassador. He retired from public life after the *coup d'état*.

BEDEAU, MARIE ALPHONSE (1804–1863), general, most of whose career was spent in Algeria. In command in Paris in February 1848, he displayed little energy in suppressing the insurrection.

BEUGNOT, AUGUSTE, COMTE DE (1797–1865), elected deputy to the constituent assembly for the Haute-Marne in 1848. He retired from public life after the *coup d'état*.

BLANC, LOUIS (1811–1882), journalist, historian and politician. In 1839 he published *L'Organisation du Travail*, arguing in favour of co-operation to replace competition as the motive force in industry. He worked on the newspaper *La Réforme* in the 1840s, was a member of the provisional government and president of the Luxembourg commission. Accused of complicity in the demonstration of 15 May 1848, he fled into exile where he remained until 1870.

BLANQUI, LOUIS AUGUSTE (1805–1881), leading Revolutionary figure during the July Monarchy. He was imprisoned after the Paris insurrection of 1839. After the February Revolution he organized the Société républicaine centrale. Arrested for complicity in the demonstration of 15 May 1848, he was imprisoned until 1859.

BONFILS, LOUIS ANTOINE (1814–18?), master hosier at Belleville. Member in 1848 of the Club des Montagnards de Belleville. On 23 June he was among the insurgents at the barrière de la Courtille. Arrested on 26 June carrying powder, he was transported, then amnestied in June 1849.

CASTELLANE, BONIFACE, COMTE DE (1788–1862), maréchal of France after 1852. He took part in the campaigns of empire, but was retired by the provisional government in 1848. He participated in the *coup d'état* of 1851, having been recalled to active service by Louis-Napoléon in 1849.

CAUSSIDIÈRE, LOUIS MARC (1808–1861), silk worker, then merchant, at Lyon where he participated in risings in 1831 and 1834. Sentenced to twenty years' imprisonment, he was amnestied in 1837. He worked as a journalist on *La Réforme*, and became prefect of police at Paris following the February Revolution. He was elected to the constituent assembly by the Seine, but, unwilling to repress the insurrection of 15 May, he was forced to resign as prefect and deputy. He was forced into exile following the June insurrection for suspected complicity.

CAVAIGNAC, LOUIS EUGENE (1802–1857), general, spending much of his military career in Algeria. After the February Revolution he was appointed governor-general of Algeria. Elected to the constituent assembly by the Lot, he became minister of war in May. During the June days he was given dictatorial powers by the assembly to crush the insurrection. He was head of a moderate Republican ministry until the success of Louis-Napoléon thwarted his bid for the presidency.

CHARRAS, JEAN-BAPTISTE (1810–1865), soldier and republican politician. Deputy of Puy-de-Dôme in 1848, he served as under-secretary of state at the ministry of war and was active in suppressing the June insurrection. He was exiled following the *coup d'état*.

JOIGNEAU, PIERRE (1815–1892), son of a prosperous peasant and carter. A member of secret societies and a Republican publicist in Paris in the 1830s, he was imprisoned from 1839 to 1842. He then returned to Beaune to continue his activities, and was elected to the constituent and legislative assemblies. He was editor of *La Réforme* from June 1848, and of the newspaper *La Feuille du Village* (October 1849–December 1851), which was directed toward peasants.

LAMARTINE, ALPHONSE DE (1790–1869), poet and politician, elected deputy of Bergues (Nord) in 1833 and then of Mâcon in 1839. He opposed government immobilism, and was active in the campaign for constitutional reform. In February 1848 he became member of the provisional government responsible for foreign affairs.

LEDRU-ROLLIN, ALEXANDRE AUGUSTE (1807–1874), Republican lawyer, prominent in political trials during the July Monarchy. Elected deputy for Le Mans in 1841, he was to the extreme Left of the radicals, and was a proponent of universal suffrage and social reform. Minister of the interior in the provisional government, and a member of the executive commission established in May, he supported the repression of the June insurrection. He went into exile following the demonstration in June 1849.

LE FLÔ, ADOLPHE CHARLES (1804–1887), general serving in Algeria. Elected to the constituent assembly in 1848, he opposed Louis-Napoléon, and was exiled between 1851 and 1857.

MONTALEMBERT, CHARLES FORBES DE (1810–1870), a leader during the July Monarchy of liberal Catholics, pleading the case of freedom for the Church to develop its role in popular education. He represented the Doubs in the constituent assembly. He approved the repression of June 1848, becoming increasingly anti-democratic and a supporter of Louis-Napoléon. Soon after the *coup d'état* he moved into opposition.

MORNY, CHARLES DE (1811–1865), natural son of General Flahaut, and Queen Hortense, and therefore half-brother to Louis-Napoléon. From 1830 to 1838 he was an army officer; he served as deputy of Puy-de-Dôme in 1842–48 and in 1849. He helped organize the *coup d'état*, after which he became minister of the interior. He was president of the Corps Législatif in 1854–65. He combined his political career with financial speculation.

NADAUD, MARTIN (1815–1898), mason from the Limousin who was a migrant worker in Paris during the July Monarchy. He moved in Republican and socialist circles in the 1840s, and was elected to the legislative assembly by the Creuse in May 1849. A leader of the parliamentary Montagne after 13 June 1849, he was arrested on 1 December 1851 and exiled until 1870.

PELISSIER, AIMABLE JEAN JACQUES (1794–1854), general whose active service was mainly in Algeria.

SAINT-ARNAUD, ACHILLE LEROY DE (1798–1854), minister of war in 1852, he assured the military success of the *coup d'état*. He was appointed maréchal in 1852.

STERN, DANIEL, pseudonym of MARIE DE FLAVIGNY, comtesse d'Agoult (1805–1876), author of historical and philosophical studies.

THIERS, ADOLPHE (1797–1877), lawyer, historian, journalist and politician. A leader of opposition to Charles X, he was minister of the interior (1832–34), minister for foreign affairs and head of government (February–August 1836, and March–October 1840). He favoured the crushing of the insurrection in Paris in February 1848. A deputy in the constituent assembly, he presided over the Comité de la rue de Poitiers, which organized the Conservative 'party of order'. He supported Louis-Napoléon in December 1848 and played a leading role in formulating the education law of 1850. He was exiled in 1852.

TOCQUEVILLE, CHARLES ALEXIS HENRI CLEREL DE (1805–1859), writer, opponent of Guizot, favouring democratic reforms. He was minister for foreign affairs at the time of the Roman expedition (1849).

Sources of the documents

The documents included in this collection were obtained from the following sources:

Archives nationales, Paris.
Archives historiques du Ministère de la Guerre (Vincennes).
Archives of the Paris Prefecture of Police.
Bibliothèque nationale newspaper collection.
Bulletin de lois de la République française.
Compte rendu des séances de l'Assemblée nationale, 1848–52.
Rapport de la commission d'enquête sur l'insurrection qui a éclate dans la journée du 23 juin et sur les événements du 15 mai.
Les Murailles révolutionnaires de 1848.

R. Apponyi   *De la révolution au coup d'état* Geneva
                            1948
O. Barrot   *Mémoires posthumes* vols. II, III, IV,
                            Paris 1875–76

J. Bergier	*Le Journal d'un bourgeois de Lyon en 1848* Paris (undated)
L. Blanc	*Révélations historiques* Leipzig 1859
Maréchal d'Isly Bugeaud	*Veillées d'une chaumière de la Vendée* Lyon 1849
Maréchal de Castellane	*Journal*, vol. IV, Paris 1896
Caussidière	*Mémoires*, 2 vols. London 1848
V. Considérant	*Journée du 13 Juin, 1849. Simples explications à mes amis et à mes commettants* Paris 1849
General Marquis A. d'Hautpoul	*Mémoires* Paris 1906
L. de la Hodde	*Histoire des sociétés secrètes et du parti républicain de 1830 à 1848* Paris 1850
P. Joigneaux	*Souvenirs historiques* Paris 1898
Earl of Kerry (ed.)	*The Secret of the Coup d'État* London 1924
A. de Lamartine	*Histoire de la révolution de 1848* 2 vols. Paris 1852 (English transl. *History of the Revolution of 1848* London 1852)
A. Lucas	*Les clubs et les clubistes* Paris 1851
Martinelli	*Un Mot sur la situation* Bordeaux 1848
K. Marx	*The Eighteenth Brumaire of Louis Bonaparte* (Marx-Engels Selected Works, vol. I), Moscow 1962
P. Mayer	*Histoire du deux décembre* Paris 1852
L. Mènard	*Prologue d'une révolution* Paris 1849
M. Nadaud	*Mémoires de Léonard* Paris 1948
Lord Normanby	*Journal of the Year of Revolution* 2 vols. London 1851
Maréchal Pélissier	*Aspects de la vie politique et militaire en France à travers la correspondance reçue par le maréchal Pélissier* (eds. P. Guiral, R. Brunon), Paris 1971
P.-J. Proudhon	*Les Confessions d'un révolutionnaire* Paris 1929
C. de Rémusat	*Mémoires de ma vie* vol. IV, Paris 1962
M. A. Romieu	*Le Spectre rouge de 1852* Berlin 1851
D. Stern	*Histoire de la Révolution de 1848* 3 vols. Paris 1850–52
E. Ténot	*La Province en décembre 1851* Paris 1868

A. de Tocqueville

Recollections London 1970
Œuvres complètes vols. VI (1), VIII (2),
IX, Paris 1959–67

ewspapers cited

L'Aimable Faubourien	(Revolutionary Republican)
L'Ami du Peuple	(Conservative, directed at the masses)
Le Constitutionnel	(Conservative, rallied to Louis-Napoléon in 1848)
Le Courrier du Tarn-et-Garonne	(Conservative, published at Montauban)
La Gazette de France	(Legitimist)
La Liberté	(Conservative, published at Rouen)
Le Mémorial Bordelais	(Conservative, published at Bordeaux)
Le National	(Moderate Republican, becoming more Radical following the election of Bonaparte)
Le Peuple Souverain	(successor to *Le Peuple*, founded by P.-J. Proudhon)
La Presse	(Conservative)
La Réforme	(Radical Republican)
La Révolution	(Radical Republican)
L'Union	(Legitimist)
La Vraie République	(Radical Republican)

uggested further reading

GENERAL

M. Agulhon	*1848 ou l'apprentissage de la République 1848–1852* Paris 1973
G. Duveau	*1848: The Making of a Revolution* London 1967
F. A. da Luna	*The French Republic under Cavaignac* Princeton 1969
R. D. Price	*The French Second Republic* London, Ithaca, N.Y. 1972
P. Vigier	*La Seconde République* Paris 1967

MORE SPECIALIZED

M. Agulhon	*La République au village* Paris 1970 *Une Ville ouvrière au temps du socialisme utopique. Toulon de 1815 à 1851* Paris 1970

A. Armengaud	*Les Populations de l'est–Aquitain au début de l'époque contemporaine* Paris 1961
P. Bastid	*Doctrines et institutions politiques de la Seconde République* 2 vols. Paris 1945
P. Chalmin *et al.*	*L'Armée et la Seconde République* Paris 1955
G. Dupeux	*Aspects de l'histoire sociale et politique du Loir-et-Cher* Paris 1962
R. Gossez	*Les Ouvriers de Paris* Paris 1967
E. Labrousse (ed.)	*Aspects de la crise et de la depression de l'économie française au milieu du 19ᵉ siècle* Paris 1956
C. Marcilhacy	*Le Diocèse d'Orléans au milieu du 19ᵉ siècle* Paris 1964
P. Pierrard	*La Vie ouvrière a Lille sous le Second Empire* Paris 1965
R. Thabault	*Education and Change in a Village Community* London 1971
A. J. Tudesq	*Les Grands Notables en France (1840–1849): Étude historique d'une psychologie sociale* 2 vols. Paris 1964
	L'Election présidentielle de Louis-Napoléon Bonaparte, 10 décembre, 1848 Paris 1965
J. Vidalenc	*Le Peuple des campagnes* Paris 1969
P. Vigier	*La Seconde République dans la région alpine* 2 vols. Paris 1963

MEMOIRS

Maréchal de Castellane	*Journal*, vol. IV, Paris 1896
M. Nadaud	*Mémoires de Léonard, ancien garçon maçon* Paris 1895
C. de Rémusat	*Mémoires de ma vie*, vol. IV, Paris 1962
A. de Tocqueville	*Recollections* London 1970

Index

Page numbers in italics refer to illustrations

ALAIS 141
Albert 25, *27*, 35, 69, 98
Allier 48, 161
Amiens 112
André, Etienne 168
Apponyi, R. 78, 79, *153*, 175
Arago *27*
Arbas 125
Ardèche 48, 163
Association Démocratique des Amis de la Constitution 137
L'Atelier 21, 63
Aube 178
Authier, Mlle 82
Azémar 134

BABEUF 172
Baciot 91
Bâgé-le-Chatel 170
Barbès, Armand *32, 33*, 106, 114, 182
Barrot, Odilon 40, 44, 45, 53, 56, 57, 75, 89, 118, 182
Baudin, Alphonse *47*
Bayonne 160
Baze 154
Beaucaire 125
Beaumont, Gustave de 182
Bedeau, Marie Alphonse 154, 156, 182
Beisser 141
Beugnot, Auguste, Comte de 141, 182

Béziers '161–2, 164–5
Blanc, Louis 24, *27*, 31, 68, 69, 112, 117, 182, 183
Blanqui, Adolphe 14
Blanqui, Auguste 72, 77
Bonald, Cardinal de 68
Bonfils, Louis Antoine 183
Bonnal 134
Borne, Antoine 171
Bosquet, Louis 110
Boudin, Louis-Martin 170
Bourelly, Commandant 162
Bouveyron 92
Breda, Raymond de 158
Brichet 111
Brossette 122
Bugeaud, Maréchal 66, 135

CABET, Etienne 21, 117
Cadiot 87
Castellane, Boniface, Comte de 79, 127, 139, 146–8, 149, 158, 173, 183
Caumette, François 168
Caussidière, Louis Marc 55, 99, 183
Cavaignac, Louis Eugène 35, 36, 37, *37*, 40, *40*, 112, 129, 131, 154, 183
Central Club for the Rights of Man 97
Châlons 113
Chambert, Maxime 165, 168

Changarnier, General 45, 154
Charente 91
Charras, Jean-Baptiste 154, 156, 183
Chucasse, André-Pierre 165
Club of Clubs 85–6
Clubs, influence of 75–6
Coffin, Justin-Henri 110
Colmar 151
Colombier, François 169
Communism, fear of 89
Considerant, Victor 138
Le Constitutionnel 68, 73, 102, 103, 127, 133, 144–5, 146, 153, 177
Corbuet, Captain 110
Coup d'état, 1851 46–50, 153, 154–81
Crémieux, Adolphe 25, *27*

DAHUBERT 87
Decceau 91
Dôle 88
Draguignan 125
Dudrage, Simon 166–8
Dufaure 157
Duval 89

EDUCATION LAW 42, 142
Elections, April 1848 30, 31, 85–96; December 1848 40–1, 128–30; April 1849 134–5; March 1850 144; April 1850 44

FALLOUX, Comte de 102
Famberta 94
February Revolution, 1848 24, 52–106
Forest laws and disorders 81–2, 125
Fous, Prosper 169

GARD 48, 163
Garnier-Pagès, Louis 25, *27*, 102

La Gazette de France 64
Gers 48, 124
Goldenberg, G. 82–3
Goudchaux 103
Grenoble 159
Grimal 165
Guichard 88

HAUTPOUL, Alphonse d' 99
Hayange 156

JARRY 110
Joigneaux, Pierre 76, 183–4
Joubert 109
June Insurrection 33–5, *35*, 107–17

LA CORBIÈRE 91
Lacoste 90
La Hodde, Lucien de 58
Lamartine, Alphonse de 25, *27*, *40*, 52–4, 55–8, 59–62, 67, *67*, 70, 84, 101, 107, 184
Lamoricière 154
Laponneraye 140
La Rochejaquelein, de 157
Lauze, Isaac 166
Lavollée 18
Ledru-Rollin, Alexandre 25, *27*, 33, 36, 40, *40*, 41, 80, 135, 184
Le Flô, Adolphe Charles 144, 154, 184
Leroux, Pierre 117
L'Eure, Dupont de *27*
Lherbette 127
La Liberté 120
Lignon, Marcel 169
Lignon, Urban 170
Limousin 159
Lot-et-Garonne 48, 162
Louis-Napoléon 37, *39*, 40, *40*, 42, 44, 45, 46, 48, 50–1, 105, 107, 118, 129, 131, 142–5, 152, 155, 174, 175, 178, *180*, 181

Louis-Philippe 56, 60–1, 62, 75
Lunel 83
Luxembourg Commission 69
Lyon 17, 25, 123, 129, 146, 149,
    157, 158, 178

Mâcon 170–1
Marie, Pierre 25, 27
Marrast, Armand 25, 27
Marseilles 114–15, 157
Martinelli, Jules 132
Marx, Karl 33, 35, 128, 181
Mauril, Antoine 166
Mayer, P. 177
Mémorial Bordelais 122
Ménard, Louis 71
Mereaux 88
Meuse 44
Mijanès 81–2
Molé 57, 132, 153
Mollin 91
Le Moniteur 68, 69, 70, 81, 84–5
Montagne 36, 42
Montalembert 122, 126, 178, 184
Montpellier 159
Morny, Charles de 136, 155, 184
Morteau 126
Mulhouse 18, 156
Les Murailles révolutionnaires de
    1848 63–4, 68, 70, 73, 74

Nadaud, Martin 75, 184
Le National 24, 33, 59, 60, 62, 98,
    110, 111, 112, 116, 117, 132, 137,
    145
National Guard 43, 56, 65
National workshops 28, 28, 30, 33,
    68, 101–5, 101, 107
Nièvre 48, 163
Nîmes 84
Nord 44
Normanby, Lord 130

Pagany 129
Panat, de 157
Paris, uprising of February 1848
    24, 25, 55–6; demonstration of
    March 1848 30, 84–5; demon-
    stration of May 1848 98–100;
    June insurrection, 1848 33–5,
    107–17; demonstration of June
    1849 42; electoral law of 1850
    44; 1851 coup d'état in 46, 156–7;
    et passim
Pech, Jean 165, 169
Pelissier, Aimable Jean Jacques 184
Peu 89
Le Peuple Souverain 76
Prat 89, 90
Proudhon, P.-J. 71, 117
Provisional government 1848,
    comes to power 62–8; and the
    demonstration of March 1848
    84–5; lack of confidence in 78–9;
    measures of 68–71

Ramy, Dominique 169
Raspail 40, 117
La Réforme 24, 33, 59, 62, 72, 75,
    96, 98, 116, 126, 132, 134
Rémusat, Charles de 62, 66, 78, 98,
    120, 136, 143
La Révolution 150, 152
Revolution (1789) 29
Revolution (1792) 95
Revolution (1830) 23, 63
Rhône 41, 44, 45
Ribeauvillé 141
Robespierre 49, 89
Rochefort 140
Rodier 87
Romieu, M. A. 153
Rosières 84
Rothschild, James de 23
Rouen 25, 31, 87
Roux 165

Sabatier 134
Saint-Arnaud, A. L. de 45, 154, 185
Saône 14, 41
Saône-et-Loire 48, 160
Sarthe 48
Seine Inférieure 44
Semur 83
Solidarité républicaine 37, 42, 123–4
Stern, Daniel 75, 185
Stevenot 90

Tax, forty-five-centime 31, 80–1, 88–9, 124–6, 127, 128
Thiers, Adolphe 37, 40, 56, 57, 130, 132, 154, 185
Tocqueville, Alexis de 64–5, 79, 94, 95, 97, 118, 127, 131, 133, 136, 143, 180, 185

Tudesq, A. J. 22

L'Union 176

Vachez 117
Var 48, 160–1
Vaucluse 163
Vauvert 164
La Voix de Peuple 142
La Vraie République 76, 96

Workers, national workshops 28, 28, 30, 33, 68, 101–5, 101, 107; promise of new era for 28, 72–3; right to work 28, 68; working hours 28, 69–70

Yonne 48

Sources of the illustrations

Art Institute of Chicago (Henry Field Memorial Collection) p. 10 (*bottom*); Bibliothèque Nationale pp. 14, 26, 27 (*top*), 27 (*bottom*), 35, 38, 43 (*bottom left*), 47 (*top left*), 65, 67 (*bottom*), 71, 95, 139, 180; British Museum p. 78; Bulloz pp. 32 (*top*), 47 (*bottom*); *Illustrated London News* frontispiece, pp. 28, 29, 30, 50, 61, 179; *Illustration* p. 15; *Journal pour rire* pp. 39 (*top*), 101, 130, 138, 148, 149; Musée Carnavalet pp. 19, 25, 43 (*top*), 47 (*bottom*), 53, 67 (*top*); Musée de Versailles p. 37; *Punch* p. 40; *Revue Comique* pp. 21, 76; Roger-Viollet p. 10 (*top*); Service de documentation photographique p. 37.